Your Towns and Cities in the Great War

Wigan
in the Great War

Your Towns and Cities in the Great War

Wigan
in the Great War

Stephen McGreal

Pen & Sword
MILITARY

First published in Great Britain in 2016 by
PEN & SWORD MILITARY
an imprint of
Pen and Sword Books Ltd
47 Church Street
Barnsley
South Yorkshire S70 2AS

ISBN 978 1 47383 478 1

A CIP record for this book is available from the British Library

Printed and bound in England
by CPI Group (UK) Ltd, Croydon, CR0 4YY

Typeset in Times New Roman by Chic Graphics

Pen & Sword Books Ltd incorporates the imprints of
Pen & Sword Archaeology, Atlas, Aviation, Battleground, Discovery,
Family History, History, Maritime, Military, Naval, Politics, Railways,
Select, Social History, Transport, True Crime, Claymore Press,
Frontline Books, Leo Cooper, Praetorian Press, Remember When,
Seaforth Publishing and Wharncliffe.

For a complete list of Pen and Sword titles please contact
Pen and Sword Books Limited
47 Church Street, Barnsley, South Yorkshire, S70 2AS, England
E-mail: enquiries@pen-and-sword.co.uk
Website: www.pen-and-sword.co.uk

Contents

Preface

The focus of commemoration during the centenary years of the First World War has concentrated on the war of attrition and the appalling cost in human life suffered by all belligerents. The casualty figures under-standably highlight the consequences of the war of attrition, and generally omit any reference to the civilians killed on the home fronts due to enemy action. From 1914, defenceless women and children endured for the first time the horror of air raids and naval bombardments, as well as black outs and food rationing. Dining tables across the land soon had vacant seats as men responded to Kitchener's call to arms or compulsory military service; many failed to return or came home broken in body or mind. In France, Britain's small professional army faced a David and Goliath battle but lacked the deadly sling shot to smite the most powerful military machine in the world – Germany.

The old Wigan coat of arms.

An unprecedented arms race ensued, as all nations strove to deliver the tools and manpower so desperately needed in the front line. In doing so, the home front responded magnificently to the call 'Feed the Guns'; the British war effort would involve, in one form or other, almost every inhabitant over school age. In 1798 income tax was implemented in Britain to finance weapons and equipment for the Napoleonic wars, but taxation alone was inadequate to finance a twentieth century mechanised war. In the true spirit of philanthropy, through the dark days of fear and hardship, local communities established or supported thousands of appeal funds which were set up for every conceivable patriotic cause. The Great War was greatly financed by people who asked for and received nothing whatsoever from the state, but were still inspired by patriotism and allegiance to the king and the belief in their cause.

Hopefully this concise work delivers an appropriate reflection of the contribution to victory delivered by the population of Wigan and district. The author has refrained from including copious local military obituaries as they are available on the Wigan archives website.

Stephen McGreal
September 2015

A poignant section of Wigan Cemetery.

Acknowledgements

To faithfully encompass the conditions prevailing upon the home front, the author has extensively consulted contemporary (Press Bureau censored) regional newspapers. The author wishes to thank the following: the production team at Pen and Sword publishers, Alex Miller and Rita Musa and her helpful colleagues at Wigan Archives service where I spent many hours scouring Council Minutes and also microfilm versions of the *Wigan Observer and District Advertiser* and the *Wigan Examiner*.

I am also grateful to Wigan Archives and Library Services (WA&LS) for providing the images on pages 83, 88 and 128.

Introduction

Between Liverpool and Manchester lies the ancient parish of Wigan comprising fourteen townships. The ancient and loyal borough of Wigan is the oldest in Lancashire and one of the oldest in England. The first settlers are thought to be the Brigantes, territorially the largest Celtic tribe in Britain and the namesakes of the supporters' club of the highly successful Wigan Warriors Rugby League Football Club.

In the 1930s booklet *Ancient and Loyal Wigan*, Arthur J. Hawkes FSA suggests the name Wigan may have derived from the Anglo-Saxon *weg*, meaning a way or road, which with the plural ending *en* or *an* would signify a crossroads. The town's Anglo-Saxon heritage is clear from the word 'gate' instead of street for the four principal thoroughfares.

Standishgate.

In the first century the area was conquered by the Romans who established six stations in Lancashire and it is suggested they knew Wigan as Coccium. Supporting evidence includes its location on principal Roman highways, pottery and coins discovered in the centre of town, a Roman Mithraic temple found beneath the parish church and traces of a large Roman property and bath house.

Wigan is not mentioned in the 1086 Domesday Book but may be included in the Neweton barony (modern Newton-le-Willows) as the church mentioned is thought to be Wigan Parish Church. In 1100 the flourishing town of Wigan was granted a borough charter by Henry I and in 1189 the name of the rector of Wigan is recorded, his successors were lords of the manor of Wigan until the nineteenth century.

In 1246 King Henry III granted a royal charter affording wide powers of self government and the charter of 1257 granted the rector permission to hold a weekly Monday market and two annual fairs.

In 1315 Wigan was the centre of the Banastre Rebellion, an uprising against the Earl of Lancaster and his supporters. Eventually two of the knights were betrayed and beheaded at Charnock Richard. Sir William Bradshaigh fled after being outlawed for conniving in the death of Sir Henry Bury. After the 1322 execution of the Earl of Lancaster, a pardoned Bradshaigh returned home. But, believing her husband dead Lady Mabel, heiress of Haigh and Blackrod, had bigamously married Sir Henry Teuthor who was murdered by the indignant Bradshaigh. As penance for her bigamy the remorseful Lady Mabel is reputed to have walked barefoot weekly from Haigh Hall to a stone wayside marker in Standishgate subsequently known as Mab's Cross. In 1333 Bradshaigh was murdered and Lady Mabel passed the Haigh estate onto male Bradshaigh or Bradshaghe relations so it remained in the family until the 1785 death of the fourth baronet. The estate was inherited by his great-niece Elizabeth Dalrymple, wife of Alexander Lindsay, the 6th Earl of Balcarres.

Throughout the medieval period Wigan prospered and, following the 1450 discovery of the easily combustible cannel coal on the Bradshaigh estate, simple mining operations commenced. The Wars of the Roses (1455-1487), fought between Lancastrian and York forces, bypassed Wigan but archers were mustered, a hark back to that time being Hardybutts, off Scholefield Lane.

By 1536 the town was described as 'paved as big as Warrington and better builded'.

Mab's Cross.

During the English Civil War (1642-1651) Wigan was the Royalist Headquarters for the North West counties, probably due to the King's General, James Stanley, 7th Earl of Derby residing in the nearby Lathom House. On seven occasions Parliamentarian forces plundered Wigan; the treasury in the Old Moot Hall was once looted to the extent of £20,000 and the entire mayoral regalia stolen.

In the final phase of the conflict the Earl of Derby arrived from the Isle of Man with 300 Manxmen and joined the Royalist forces gathering in Lancashire. Intending to make Wigan his headquarters, the earl and 1,500 men were in sight of the town when 3,000

A representation of the sixteenth century Moot Hall, including a market cross, is included in the old borough seal.

Parliamentarians commanded by Colonel Lilburn were observed on the rising banks of the River Douglas to his left with others lining the hedges on his right. On 25 August 1651 the Royalists were defeated in the Battle of Wigan Lane during which the Earl of Derby had two horses shot from under him and was severely wounded. The earl fled into Wigan, hiding overnight in the Dog Inn; the fleeing Royalist army was hunted down and killed. A monument at the junction of Monument Road and Wigan Lane marks the place where the Royalist Major General Thomas Tyldesley fell during the battle.

Monument Park

Throughout the Industrial Revolution circa 1760 to 1830 Wigan's prosperity flourished. The employment opportunities offered by the town's three great industries, coal, cotton and iron, created a sharp rise in the population. The canals became the life blood of the Industrial Revolution. The financially troubled canalisation of part of the River Douglas commenced in the 1740s, followed by the diversion of the Leeds and Liverpool canal, to ease the transportation of Lancashire cloth and food stuffs to Liverpool. Construction resumed in the 1790s and was completed in 1816; the waterway now became the primary route for transporting coal to Leeds and Liverpool.

The transport infrastructure further improved during the 1830s when Wigan became one of the first towns to be linked by a railway. The line had connections to the Preston and the Manchester and Liverpool Railway. It was said that Britain's bread hangs by Lancashire's thread and Wigan was no exception for by 1818 the Wallgate part of Wigan had eight huge cotton mills and by 1829 thirty-two steam engines operated in them. The town became a dominant force in the cotton industry.

By 1829 thirsty workers could slake their thirst in one of Wigan's sixty-eight inns. There would be no shortage of customers for by 1854 there were fifty-four collieries in and around the town. Three years later Wigan opened Britain's second School of Mines. By the end of the nineteenth century Wigan was one of the most important mining centres in the country with upwards of 1,000 pit shafts within 5 miles of Wigan centre. In close proximity to the town centre stands Wigan Pier. No.1 Terminus Warehouse was constructed in 1777 and in the 1890s the construction of Warehouse No.2 and No.3 created extra storage space for cargoes of grain, sugar, dried fruit, cotton etc.

In 1878, the *Wigan Examiner* graphically described the town thus: 'Wigan is a grim emporium of labour and industry; it is devoid of natural beauties and the atmosphere is polluted by the serpentine and cloud like columns of smoke which are vomited from the huge chimneys by which we are surrounded.'

In 1911 the town had a population of 89,152 and Great Britain was at the height of her economic and colonial power. To most citizens it would have been incomprehensible to consider that the 28 June 1914

Wigan Pier where dry goods were loaded or unloaded beneath the canopy.

assassination of the Archduke Franz Ferdinand and his wife in Sarajevo, the capital of Bosnia, would precipitate a chain of events culminating in the outbreak of the Great War, now generally known as the First World War. The road to Armageddon was merely precipitated by the murder, for the root causes of the conflict are diverse, the primary causes being nationalistic ambitions, insecurity, expansion of territory and military brinkmanship.

Seeking reparations for the murders by Bosnian Serb assassins, Austria-Hungary, prompted by Germany, made a series of uncompromising demands on Serbia which agreed to most of the demands, except for the issue of sovereignty. The British proposed a conference to arbitrate the issues but this was declined by Austria-Hungary, and, as a result, on 28 July 1914, war was declared on Serbia. Against such an incursion the European powers were linked by international treaties of support. The next day Russia commenced mobilising troops to come to the aid of her Serbian ally. Russia refused German demands to demobilise which led to the 1 August declaration of war; two days later Germany declared war on France.

Long-standing German preparations for war required the army to rapidly advance in a great sweeping arc through France; in doing so Paris would fall, prompting the capitulation of France. To do so, Germany required free passage of its troops through neutral Belgium. The German march to victory was intended to be accomplished before Russia could fully deploy her troops, thus preventing an unsustainable war on two fronts.

On 3 August 1914, plucky Belgium refused German demands of

passage across their nation but the following day Germany entered Belgium. It was a calculated gamble, for Germany doubted Britain would honour the treaty to protect Belgium neutrality, especially as the British royal family were of German extraction. But on 4 August Britain declared war in compliance with what the Germans scathingly called 'a scrap of paper'. A war that many had thought probable came to fruition from 11pm (midnight German time).

BRAVO, BELGIUM!

This cartoon, reproduced by special permission of the proprietors of "Punch," admirably expresses the true spirit of the Belgians' resistance to German aggression.

This Punch cartoon expresses the true spirit of the Belgians' resistance to German aggression.

CHAPTER 1

1914
Eager for a Fight

The prospect of war was disconcerting to the British, who envisaged if anything, a brief campaign in Europe, culminating in the inevitable British victory. The depressing newspaper headlines dampened the bank holiday atmosphere but most people resolved to enjoy the long weekend. The local theatre adverts for Saturday, 4 August included 'A Fool in Paradise', offered by the Royal Court Theatre, Wigan where all Territorial soldiers were admitted half price. The Pavilion, Library Street offered 'The Wages of Crime', billed as the exclusive and expensive booking of the greatest and most sensational drama ever filmed. Not to be outdone the Hippodrome offered the international idol and favourite of England and America. Miss Zona Vevey, who had a peerless singing voice, was Britain's daintiest comedienne and engaged by the Hippodrome at the largest salary ever paid to any individual artiste.

Fiscal arrangements elsewhere were cause for concern. To prevent a run on the financial institutions, the bank holiday was extended for several days, but it only applied to banks. This gave banks and financial institutions time to ascertain how they stood, and to give the Government time to prepare and issue one pound and ten shilling notes in order that the banks should be able to meet demands on them for smaller currency than five pound notes. The new notes, which were payable in gold at the bank, were ready to the extent of £3,000,000 on

7 August, when the banks re-opened. Subsequent issues of notes at the rate of £5,000,000 a day relieved the pressure on London. On 10 August, over £2,600,000 of United States gold was received in London. The problem of providing currency was successfully met by the issue of the new notes.

£1 Badge

The new fiscal measures reflected the concerns of Wigan's Mayor who made the following request:

'I appeal to all the inhabitants of Wigan to support their King and country by keeping calm and refraining from any excitement of any kind. All inhabitants please remember that they can materially help their country's interest by withdrawing as little money as possible from circulation, by not buying more food or other provisions than in ordinary times'.

There was no panic, for the townspeople had received the declaration of war in a manner that indicated it was expected, although the mobilization of military reservists and part-time territorial soldiers did attract a great deal of attention. By Tuesday evening the Wigan streets were thronged with inhabitants and a crowd gathered around the General Post Office to read the various mobilization orders, including those for the Wigan Territorials known as the 5th Manchester Regiment (5/Manchester), who had just returned from their annual camp at Stalybridge.

The officer commanding this unit of part-time soldiers, Colonel W.S. France VD (Volunteer Decoration), immediately appealed for recruits for the Wigan battalion to enable it to proceed to its war station at full strength. In response, on Tuesday evening large numbers of recruits presented themselves at Powell Street Drill Hall where, after passing medical examinations, fifty recruits attested (joined up); the battalion rapidly reached full strength. All members were now subject to military law, failure to attend for assembly or embodiment without reasonable excuse could lead to a charge of desertion and a court martial.

On the morning of Friday, 7 August considerable enthusiasm was shown when the Leigh Territorials comprising 124 men and three officers drew up in front of Leigh Town Hall where the Mayor bade them God-speed and assured corporation employees their places would be kept open for them. He urged other employers to follow suit. On the conclusion of the civic parade, the company marched to Wigan where they were joined in the evening by the Atherton and Patricroft companies thereby completing the muster of the 5/Manchester. Of the eight companies A, B, C, D and E represented Wigan, F Company (Eccles), G Company (Leigh) and H Company (Atherton). Besides the Drill Hall the following schools served as billets: Wesleyan, St John's, St Paul's, St Mary's and St George's Old Club, each entrance being guarded by soldiers with bayonets.

Most leaders asserted the conflagration would be brief, but the recently appointed Secretary of War, Lord Kitchener, vehemently

A Spring Bank Wigan photographer recorded for posterity what appear to be members of an East Lancashire Regiment group of Territorials.

disagreed. On 8 August he called for 100,000 volunteers between the ages of nineteen and thirty to join the British Army; the response was phenomenal. Within a fortnight, in a wave of patriotism, 100,000 men of all social classes enlisted to serve for the duration of a war they expected to be satisfactorily concluded by Christmas 1914.

As the military were largely dependent on equine horsepower for transportation, Remount Officers, in accordance with the Army Act Impressments Order, began commandeering draft horses and any deemed suitable as officers' mounts. A few days after war broke out, remount officers visited Wigan and district stables; no fewer than sixty-eight of Middleton and Wood's animals were commandeered and harness was procured from the Co-op and council stables.

A temporary display at the Imperial War Museum North displayed a letter from the Hewlett family of The Cottage, Haigh who were powerless to prevent two of their three horses being commandeered for front line service. Young Freda, Lionel and Poppy Hewlett sent an impassioned appeal to Lord Kitchener explaining how they were afraid for their pony Betty in case she 'may be taken for your Army' and 'Daddy says she is going to be a mother early next year'... *Please spare her.*' A sympathetic War Office administrator replied by return and reassured the children that Betty was too small (below 15 hands) for Army service and could safely remain in her paddock.

Owners of requisitioned assets were powerless; any prospect of recovering their property evaporated, for on 8 August the House of Commons passed in five minutes emergency wartime regulations for the British Government. The Defence of the Realm Act 1914 (DORA), granted the government powers to suppress published criticism, imprison without trial and to commandeer resources, including buildings or land required for the war effort; the act was regularly supplemented throughout the war.

Immediately following the start of hostilities an orchestrated wave of xenophobia swept the country; non-British citizens were now treated with suspicion. Residents were encouraged to assist the police and military authorities by keeping close observation on all foreigners (dubbed aliens), especially Germans and report any suspicious movements to the police. At Holyhead, police detained a suspected spy found sketching near the Admiralty Pier. As a result of enquiries he was identified as the Reverend Charles T. Richardson, pastor of the

English Congregational Church, Wigan, who was an innocent holidaymaker.

In compliance with a Home Office order, all Germans were required to register with the authorities. By mid-August fifteen 'sons of the Kaiser' residing in the Wigan district had signed their registration papers and could not travel more than 5 miles from their residence without police permission. Permits were also required for possession of a motor car, motor cycle or aircraft. They were further prohibited from possessing firearms, ammunition or explosives or more than three gallons of flammable liquid, any signalling apparatus, carrier or homing pigeons, and any cipher books or other means of secret correspondence.

THE IDEA—
THOUGHT I WAS A BALLY ALIEN

Bally alien.

The draconian treatment of long-standing members of the community arose from the increasing paranoia of enemy sympathisers embedded in the communities. It was feared the spies might supply military information to the enemy to facilitate invasion, provide targets for hostile airships, or sabotage the railways or water supply. To prevent contamination or disruption to Wigan Corporation's Waterworks at Worthington, Orrell and the Boar's Head service reservoir, they were watched by special constables recruited to replace called up reservists serving in the police.

Army recruitment was also in the ascendancy as Lancashire men responded to the call to arms. To aid the expansion of the army, each county was at first expected, to raise one extra war service battalion, to supplement the existing Territorial battalions. In August, Wigan raised the second line battalion 2/5 Manchester which was allocated to the 66th Division. The Territorial units existed solely for home defence, the volunteers could not be ordered overseas. However, provisions in the form of an 'Imperial Service' section were made to enable a Territorial to serve overseas if required. Those who made the declaration wore a rectangular white metal Imperial Service badge on their uniform jacket.

In Wigan, Councillor Healey, of the firm Messrs G.J. Healey and Sons provided new recruiting offices at Crawford Gallery, Bretherton's Row, off Wallgate. The boardroom of Messrs Simpson and Rogers was similarly placed at the disposal of the Wigan and District Division of the British Red Cross Society (BRCS).

The Wigan division of the St John Ambulance Brigade was formed in 1905; their membership rose dramatically following the outbreak of hostilities. During the first two months of the war, the Number 4 District, of which the Wigan Division formed a portion, supplied over 700 men for service in connection with Military Home Hospitals, Naval Hospitals and ambulance transport work in France.

In 1910 the East Lancashire Voluntary Aid Detachment (VAD) was formed with the objective of organising and training the civilian population during peacetime in readiness to assist the military

Bretherton's Row

authorities in wartime. At this juncture, the East Lancashire VADs whose unit numbers were prefixed EL, comprised:

EL50 (Parbold), Commandant Miss Rogers, The White House. This was the first VAD to be formed in the Wigan and District Division but the lack of suitable accommodation prevented the opening of a Parbold auxiliary hospital.
EL90 (Wigan), Commandant Mrs E.A. Watmough, Park View.
EL92 (Wigan) Commandant Mrs France, Bellingham House.
EL96 (Standish), Miss Brown, Mere Oaks. A reserve detachment was proposed and Doctor Buchanan, the VAD EL92 medical officer ,agreed to provide the necessary training.

The proficient volunteers of the BRCS and the Order of St John detachments registered with the War Office could now put their training to good practice.

From their headquarters in the loaned 3 King Street boardrooms the Wigan BRCS set about making the necessary arrangements to equip hospitals – the National Health Service was then non-existent. Offers of suitable houses were under consideration as leaflets were distributed requesting the gift or loan of mattresses, single sheets, blankets, enamel bowls, chairs, baths, antiseptic and all manner of medicinal requisites.

The work of the society was of two types, the first being the preparation of extra hospitals and the training of men and women; secondly there was the comforts sections for the provision of clothing and other necessities for the sick and wounded, both at the front and when invalided home. Forty comfort sections were instituted in Lancashire, with a leader in charge of each who organised sewing parties in his or her particular district. Locally the BRCS comfort section was divided into the

Red Cross nurse.

following areas: Wigan, Standish, Parbold, Haigh and Aspinall under the leadership of Lady Ratcliffe-Ellis, Mrs Hewlett, Mrs Rogers and Mrs W. Rawcliffe, respectively.

David Alexander Edward Lindsay, 27th Earl of Crawford and 10th Earl of Balcarres and chairman of the Wigan Coal and Iron Company, had extensive mining interests in the Lancashire coalfield at Haigh, near Wigan. From his family seat he forwarded the following letter to Mr Harold Sumner, chairman and assistant County Director of the Wigan and District BRCS offering what transpired to be Woodlands No.1 – the first Red Cross auxiliary hospital in the extensive area known as Western Command, covering Lancashire and parts of Cheshire.

The 27th Earl of Crawford and 10th Earl of Balcarres.

Haigh Hall, Wigan, 12 August 1914
Dear Mr Sumner,
My wife and I have been considering how best we can help the BRCS over which you preside. I think it will be serviceable if we place Woodlands at your disposal. The house is near lines of communications, convenient for the infirmary, which is the pivot of medical science in our neighbourhood, and compared with this house is central, accessible and easily supervised. I shall be glad to be responsible for its equipment as I know you have other hospitals to equip. I trust this may relieve you in one direction, and I feel confident the people of Wigan and district will by their donations and the loan of necessary items enable you to meet your obligations to the full.

We also desire to place Haigh Hall at your disposal. For the reasons which make Woodlands suitable as a hospital for urgent and serious cases, Haigh being distant and inconveniently situated is open to objections, but as a convalescent home it is admirably adapted being large, airy and quiet, it stands high and appears to be precisely what is needed for patients as they recover and require a change. I imagine we could provide accommodation for any number of patients the Wigan Red Cross Hospitals may require to send. I shall of course meet the cost, though I doubt not your society would help in collecting and preparing the equipment, as my wife is fully occupied with her naval hospital at Balcarres, and I fear may be unable to do in Lancashire as much and as often as she would wish.

Yours sincerely, Crawford and Balcarres

The offer of Woodlands (later No.1) was gratefully accepted, but it seems the offer of Haigh Hall for the use of convalescing servicemen was declined.

The war had an immediate financial impact on working class families who existed on the breadline. The average infantry soldier received one shilling (1s) a day and family men were entitled to a separation allowance, but the forms were often overlooked or processed slowly. By mid-August, War Relief Committees were formed in Wigan, Hindley, Ince and Orrell.

The mobilised East Lancashire Division (Territorial Force) concentrated in camp at Littleborough, near Rochdale. A component of the division was the Manchester Infantry Brigade comprising the 5/Manchester, 6/Manchester (from Stretford Road), 7/Manchester (Burlington Street) and 8/Manchester (from Ardwick).

To the immense relief of the 1,000 strong 5/Manchester, who had spent the past fortnight closely confined to their headquarters, on 20 August, amid emotional scenes they departed Wigan for Littleborough. The Manchester Brigade camp lay in a valley approximately triangular in shape and about a mile in length, the base of the triangle resting on the northern shore of Hollingworth lake. In the valley were camped some 5,000 Manchester Brigade men, the 3/East Lancashire Field Ambulance (Royal Army Medical Corp) and the Manchester Brigade Company of the Army Service Corps (Transport and Supply Column). The commanding officer was Brigadier General Noel Lee who had the responsibility of urgently transforming the part-time soldiers into an effective component of the 42nd (East Lancashire) Division.

The vanguard of the 100,000 strong British Expeditionary Force (BEF) reached France on 7 August. After a few weeks' concentration, the British II Corps advanced to the south-east corner of Belgium, congregating around the town of Mons where on 23 August the

The Manchesters' Camp at Hollingworth Lake.

Germans delivered a terrific onslaught. The BEF survivors were now in a headlong retreat towards the River Marne fighting continual rearguard actions. On 26 August components of the BEF made a costly stand at Le Cateau, near the town of Mons; this delaying tactic allowed the bulk of the BEF to retire unmolested. Involved in the battle were the 2/Lancashire Fusiliers whose dead included 657 Private T. Fitzpatrick, a former Wigan postman. He died on 26 August and has no known grave, consequently he is commemorated on the La Ferté-Sous-Jouarre Memorial, along with 3,739 missing soldiers. Erroneously believed to be the first Wigan death in action was Bugler Robert Reid (30), 2/Lancashire Fusiliers, who died on 13 September during the Battle of the Aisne. He was survived by a widow and one child, who resided at 50 Boswell Lane, Wigan.

The earlier press coverage of Kitchener successfully attracting his 100,000 volunteers had a negative effect on further recruitment. The indifference to the situation arose from the mistaken belief that further volunteers were not necessary, but there came sudden enlightenment which acted as a catalyst to recruitment: the censored press accounts of the retreat from Mons. Most people read through the lines and realised the gravity of the situation.

The 1 September edition of the *Wigan Observer and District Advertiser* reported:

'Major Paton, in charge of the recruiting department in Bretherton's Row, has had to increase his staff and premises. A large number of clerks have been requested to deal with the rush of recruits. No section of this community has shown its loyalty more than the miners of this neighbourhood for the greater preponderance of men are from this occupation. Other classes of working men are not strongly represented. By noon on Tuesday about 1,000 men had enlisted in Wigan and among the later comers were a large proportion of married men satisfied with the mayoral assurance that their families would be cared for. On Saturday 84 men enlisted, on Monday 174 men were despatched to various centres.

The recruits have mainly gone to the Border Regiment stationed at Carlisle, Lancashire Fusiliers at Bury, Loyal North Lancashire Regiment at Preston, South Lancashire Regiment at Warrington and the Royal Field Artillery (RFA) at Preston. Many young business men of Wigan have enlisted as troopers in cavalry regiments.'

Not everyone met the military criteria, men were rejected on medical grounds, failed to meet the 19- to 35-year-old age limit demanded for raw recruits or were prevented by their business connections. A national groundswell of a 'Dad's Army' force began to gain momentum and Doctor Wynne, Medical Officer of Wigan, offered to form a civilian corps from men over the military age limit of thirty-five. This would allow men who were unable to join the Regulars or Territorial Army an opportunity to receive military training and firing practice; youths under military age would also be accepted. The headquarters was established at Wigan Grammar School where two former Army sergeants volunteered to give instruction. On the final day of August a mass meeting was held in a packed Old Council Chamber with several hundred unable to gain admittance. The Mayor made a rousing speech and advised that men needed to put in eight hours drill a week and the first drill would take place at 7pm that evening at Springfield Park. A few names were proposed: Wigan Civic Guard and Wigan Rifle Club

Due to an unprecedented demand for uniforms the volunteer corps members had to be content with an armband bearing the initials of the royal cipher of King George V.

were rejected in preference for the Wigan Volunteer Corps.

A few days later 250 men paraded at Springfield Park and, after drill, marched back to the Market Square where they sang the National Anthem prior to being dismissed. A committee meeting followed where it was reported 320 had enlisted and paid the entrance fee. An offer was accepted from the battalion of the Church Lads Brigade for the use of All Saint's Institute and St Michael's Institute and the use of six carbines, one hour a week at each institute. The Bellingham Rifle Range's offer of use on Sundays and one afternoon in the week was also accepted. St Andrew's school playground and the Borough Police

Parade room were also offered.

The local Red Cross Division was heavily dependent on gift aid and received in mid-September a fully fitted and renovated horse ambulance donated by the Wigan Amateur Operatic Society whose president was the chairman of the Wigan BRCS. In addition, the Ladies Dress Committee and other ladies of the society forwarded large bundles of shirts, socks and other clothing to the BRCS. The local members of the VAD periodically visited Billinge Hospital to gain knowledge of hospital matters and the London and North Western Railway Company spent an autumnal Sunday morning practising unloading and loading patients from trains. They were helped by the transport section composed of members of the St John Ambulance Association and the Standish Works Fire Brigade.

On terra firma the home-front infrastructure began to gain momentum, but at sea Britain's naval dominance faced challenges. During the pre-war arms race the Royal Navy's Grand Fleet and Germany's High Seas fleet underwent rapid expansion. The British warships may have outnumbered the German fleet but the Kaiser's vessels had superior design, weaponry and heavier armoured plates. As the summer of 1914 gave way to autumn the Royal Navy patrolled the North Sea to restrict the German High Seas Fleet, shield the east coast against invasion, operate a distant blockade of German ports and guard the North Sea exits. Within this watery expanse the world's two largest navies feinted and parried blows in minor skirmishes, neither side wishing to expose their 'castles of steel' to unnecessary risk that may widen or lessen the balance of naval sea power. However this equilibrium was threatened by the success of German naval mines and submarines.

On 22 September the hospital ship *Eloby* disembarked at Liverpool the first Western Front patients destined for Western Command hospitals. On the same day, three obsolete British cruisers *Aboukir*, *Hogue* and *Cressy* were patrolling in file off the Dutch coast unaware they were covertly observed from the German submarine *U9*. In rapid succession Captain Lieutenant Otto Weddigen fired a series of torpedoes and his three targets quickly plunged to the sea-bed claiming 1,459 lives. The tragedy humiliated the Royal Navy; the submarine had come of age and altered naval tactics forever.

Each painful military setback stimulated army recruitment. At this

HMS Hogue, *one of the obsolete cruisers of the live-bait squadron.*

juncture an estimated 2,000 miners from the Wigan district had responded to Lord Kitchener's call to arms.

In mid-September crowds gathered as the Royal Field Artillery Territorials passed through Wigan to their encampment at Winstanley Park. Their horses were stabled in an old weaving shed at Taylor Brothers Mill and the stables of Middleton and Wood cab proprietors.

The martial activity at the Territorial encampment was a magnet for the curious, resulting on 9 October in an appearance at Wigan County Police Court of David Brass, a young pedlar of no fixed abode. He was charged on suspicion of being a spy attempting to obtain information at Winstanley Park, which would be directly or indirectly useful to the enemy. The prisoner, an English Jew born in London to Russian parents, loitered at the park gates hoping to sell some postcards, but was alleged to have closely examined cases of cartridges on a limber. Brass protested he was unaware the boxes contained cartridges and objected to being remanded on such flimsy evidence. Nonetheless he was remanded over the weekend and advised that the police would assist him to prove his bona fides.

More welcome visitors were the first patients for the twenty beds Woodlands Auxiliary Hospital, in the Woodlands, off Wigan Lane which opened on 6 October. The next day the *Manchester Evening News* reported that patients were transferred in three BRCS motor ambulances and two private motor cars from Whitworth Hospital, Manchester. The men, including five stretcher-cases, were assisted into the hospital by a detachment of the Wigan St John Ambulance Association. The Woodlands nursing staff were drawn from the VAD (Wigan Division) of the BRCS, and were all local ladies whose freely offered services and enthusiastic training over the past few months was being put to good use. Also in daily attendance were three Boy Scouts and two Girl Guides who assisted by running errands and carrying out mundane household chores.

Simultaneously Lord Gerard, having offered the use of Garswood Hall (now the home of Ashton-in-Makerfield Golf Course) to the War Office for the purpose of a temporary hospital for wounded soldiers, was requested to have the residence prepared promptly. The dining room was converted and appeals were made for game, fowl, fruit, vegetables and groceries. On 7 October twelve wounded soldiers from various regiments were transferred from Manchester in ambulance motor cars. A number of men from the Newton-le-Willows VAD were in attendance to assist the hospital officials to transfer the men to their new quarters. The ladies section of the VAD, which included a number of fully trained nurses, was soon carrying out nursing duties under the supervision of Mrs (Dr) Dowling officiating as superintendent.

Other women 'were out of employment owing to the war', this troubled representatives of the Wigan Distress Committee and the War Relief Fund to such an extent that the Town Clerk and Mayor met a representative of clothing manufacturers Messrs Coop and Co. Ltd., who offered training for fifty women sewing machinists. As they became more efficient they could earn higher wages; the committees accepted the offer.

Charities were now severely tested by the arrival on British shores of Belgian refugees, some in a pathetic condition, the clothes they stood in often being their sole possessions. As their numbers increased, the tide of humanity was dispersed throughout the nation where benevolent organisations provided food and shelter.

On 15 October the first Belgian refugees to be cared for and housed in Wigan arrived by train from Liverpool. The refugees, comprising five families of ten adults and eight children from Lier near Antwerp,

Britain's welcome for refugees.

received an official welcome from the Mayor, Mayoress and other dignitaries. A Belgian visitor translated the Mayor's welcoming speech and the party then passed through a large cheering crowd to a horse drawn vehicle decorated with English and Flemish flags. The crowd followed the wagonette up Wallgate to their new home at the corner of Earl Street and Upper Dicconson Street where they had a substantial evening meal. The spectators dispersed, but later the quietness was rudely interrupted 'when colliery whistles blew ominously and the rush of people in the direction of Whalley was heard in all quarters'. At Parbold, Hindley Farm House was made available to five refugees and two families comprising eleven members were housed at Prospect House, Standish.

At Hindley a refugee committee was formed. Hindley Hall, which was lent by the Hindley Golf Club, was taken over by the committee and furnished for the purpose of accommodating thirty-three refugees sent by the London War Refugee Committee. Beds and furniture were donated by the community, the Wigan Coal and Iron Company gave two loads of coal and the Hindley Boy Scouts' chrysanthemum carnival raised £108 for the Belgian Relief Fund. The first party of Hindley Hall guests comprised twenty-nine adults, two children and two babies. Days later, a further seven refugees arrived in Parbold who were accommodated in the Harrock Hill, the summer residence of a Wigan solicitor.

Meanwhile on the Western Front, the Belgian army was fighting alongside the BEF in the First Battle of Ypres. On 19 October General Sir Douglas Haig's I Corps successfully counter-attacked and effectively ended the German drive towards Calais. By now the BEF had suffered unprecedented casualties, the troops were exhausted and grimly hanging on awaiting reinforcements. Lord Kitchener mistrusted the fighting ability of the Territorials, for they existed purely as a home defence force and were not obliged to serve overseas. However, if sufficient battalion members volunteered for 'Imperial Service' they became eligible for front line service – the 5/Manchester readily accepted the challenge. Most Territorial units were assigned to guarding ports, entrenching along the east coast or safe-guarding reservoirs or railways, but several units including the 5/Manchester now prepared for disembarkation.

The 42nd (East Lancashire) Division had the distinction of being the first Territorial force to be posted overseas. The division was initially tasked with defending the Suez Canal from Turkish troops assembling in Palestine. To this end, on 10 September the 5/Manchester sailed from Southampton on the *Caledonia*.

In late October the *Wigan Observer and District Advertiser* informed readers:

'The East Lancashire Territorials along with some London Regiments are now stationed in Egypt and enjoying the novelty of the situation. They have been supplied with light drill uniforms and sun helmets, and are gradually becoming accustomed to the new diet which is necessary under the present

A novel encampment for the soldiers of the king.

climate. A great many horses died on the outward voyage and many others have suffered since due to the heat.

'The Lancashire Fusiliers Brigade is in barracks near Cairo and it was during the journey there that two men were killed by falling off the train.'

As the Lancashire troops carried out manoeuvres and extensive training, the conflict escalated on land and sea. A new chapter of frightfulness occurred on 20 October when the coal-carrying SS *Glitra* was intercepted by *U17* off the Norwegian coast. A German boarding party scuttled the vessel, making her the first Great War merchantman sunk by a submarine.

In Britain further civilian restrictions were introduced; a 21 October amendment to DORA banned fireworks and bonfires, both potential navigating beacons for any belligerent warships or airships; the timely order also prevented Bonfire Night celebrations.

On the same day new and drastic measures came into force. Under a Home Office order all German and Austrian aliens between seventeen and fifty years of age, or who were eligible for military service, were to be arrested and sent to internment camps. A considerable number of aliens who had registered under the previous order were now arrested.

The first arrested in Wigan was Gaspar Mihaly (29), a Hungarian. He arrived in town the previous week and was engaged in training performing dogs at the Hippodrome. As he was liable for military service in his country he was arrested and sent to the Lancaster Aliens Concentration Depot.

The next day Wigan County Police arrested two Germans, Max Ostoff, a collier from Haydock and a pork butcher named Max Heiss from Ashton-in-Makerfield. The retailing and processing of pork appears to have been a popular occupation for German immigrants, many of whom had long ago anglicised their names. This may explain why George Brand of 105 Diggle Street, Wigan, a pork butcher employed by Wigan Corporation, was, despite community objections, also conveyed to Lancaster for internment. Aliens not yet interned had their liberty restricted. Louis Mynakyme, a German, appeared before the magistrates for travelling more than 5 miles from his registered address without a police permit and received a staggering £40 fine.

Germans in France and Flanders were also on the move as both sides attempted to outflank each other, each abortive turning action taking the belligerents closer to the Belgian coast. The line of scattered

A quick change of name.

defences, usually little more than shallow ditches, were gradually consolidated and connected by trenches. The Western Front, comprising a 400-mile network of trenches, soon extended from the Swiss border to the North Sea.

The threat of invasion seemed likely and most volunteer units held weekly drill evenings. At Wigan the volunteers of A, B, C, D and F companies paraded on various evenings at the Drill Hall. E Company paraded at Ince, G Company at Pemberton Colliery, H Company at Orrell and, L Company at Upholland. Late in October the 500 strong Wigan Volunteer Corps paraded at the Grammar School before setting off on their inaugural route march accompanied by the Wigan Borough Reed Band and the Wigan Corporation Band. The parade marched up Wigan Lane and past the Woodlands Red Cross hospital where several wounded standing at the gateway saluted the passing battalion. After falling out at Standish market place they marched back to Wigan.

The Elms (2nd Wigan) troop of Boy Scouts were also 'doing their bit', the entertainer Miss Jennie Johns portrayed a soubrette, a vain and flirtatious comedic character. During her performances she asked her audiences to support the Cigarette Fund for soldiers at the front. Her appeals at Wigan Hippodrome broke all records allowing Miss Johns to send 50,000 cigarettes to Lancashire soldiers at the front; over £5 was also raised for Belgian refugees residing in Wigan.

Meanwhile the flames of war had reached Asia, where Germany's successful courting of Turkey induced the ailing Ottoman Empire to align with Germany. Their United Kingdom residents were now also classified as aliens and were legally required to obtain residence permits to live in any prohibited area.

Also taking up residency, albeit temporary, were wounded servicemen in a Mariebonne property, off Wigan Lane provided by Lord and Lady Crawford. Another benefactor made available The Beeches, Standish for use as an auxiliary hospital, which were respectively known as Woodlands No.2 and Woodlands No.3. They opened 16 November 1914. The trio, known as Woodlands Hospitals, Wigan, was the first such group to be opened in the country. Patients from all parts of the country and overseas dominions would pass through their doors.

Also in mid-November another recruiting rally was held in the Pavilion, Library Street, Wigan where a united call to arms was made

Mariebonne, Wigan Lane

from the platform by men of all political parties. The Mayor read aloud a telegram from Lord Derby in which he proposed 'If tonight Wigan could get 600 – 700 men to promise to join, I would undertake to secure recognition as a battalion'. This transpired to be too ambitious, as 3,095 men from Wigan and district had already joined His Majesty's forces and this was exclusive of the 1,000 local Territorials serving in Egypt.

On 14 December the first military funeral in connection with the war took place at Wigan Cemetery of a reservist called up on 5 August – 9557 Private J. Bamber, 2/Lancashire Fusiliers, of 6 Francis Street, off Prescott Street, Wigan. He was wounded in the leg at Cambrai near Mons and, despite receiving treatment at Netley Military Hospital and a lengthy furlough, he succumbed to his wounds. He was buried in a public grave in Wigan cemetery. Later the Commonwealth War Graves Commission provided a headstone bearing the legend

Private J. Bamber 2/Lancashire Fusiliers who died 20 November 1914.

'buried near this spot' as the grave is just one of a neat row of lost military graves.

Shortly after the outbreak of war, Liverpool raised the highly popular Liverpool Pals battalions comprising men who shared the bond of working for the same employers or resided in the same locality. On 5 December a big recruiting rally held in the National Schools, Standish had the object of raising a 200-strong company of men to serve together in the Wigan and District Pals. Wounded soldiers from Woodlands No.3 (Standish) occupied one side of the platform while on the other side were refugees from Prospect House. Only three per cent of the Wigan Coal and Iron Company's employees living in Standish had enlisted, while others working in similar conditions had listed to the extent of ten per cent. The recruitment figure at Clock Face was nearly thirty per cent, forty-seven per cent at St Helens and fifteen per cent at Wigan, therefore Standish was expected to increase its recruitment numbers to twenty per cent.

Men deemed to be shirking their patriotic duty were coming under increasing social pressure to enlist and even the most obstinate abstainer must have felt a twinge of conscience on witnessing wounded

Wigan Infirmary.

THE INFIRMARY WIGAN.

servicemen, of whom the Wigan Infirmary had forty-six British and two Belgian military patients. On 9 December about ninety military patients from Wigan hospitals were entertained at the Royal Court Theatre with an exhibition of colour cinematograph pictures of the fighting forces in Europe.

The risk of invasion remained an omnipotent threat driven home on 16 December 1914, when two German battle cruisers commenced a thirty-minute devastating and demoralising bombardment of Scarborough, during which seventeen civilians died and eighty were injured. The 'baby killers' of Scarborough then headed north, briefly shelling the fishing port of Whitby, and bombarded the garrisoned port of Hartlepool, where a further eighty-six civilians and seven soldiers died and 424 were injured. Instead of the much quoted 'the war would be over by Christmas' in reality it transpired that 'the war was over here by Christmas' – and with no end in sight.

The looming festive season would be dampened by the temporary or permanent absence of a loved one. Princess Mary, the third child of George V and Queen Mary, had given her name to a gift fund launched in October to provide a personal Christmas gift to 'every sailor afloat and every soldier at the front'. Nearly 500,000 embossed brass tins containing cigarettes, tobacco and clay pipe, or for non smokers writing material and acid drops, were distributed; the contents varied for colonial servicemen.

Similarly Alderman Grimshaw, the Mayor of Wigan, launched a fund to provide Christmas presents to the 3,600 children aged fourteen years or younger belonging to Wigan soldiers and sailors. Each child received an enamel medallion created by Messrs Starr & Sons Ltd., Wigan and a 1lb box of best quality chocolates supplied by Messrs Rothwell of Golborne.

Wigan Christmas badge.

The centre of the medallion bears the Wigan Borough coat of arms, above which is inscribed 'Wigan War Souvenir' and below 'Xmas 1914'. They were enclosed in an envelope bearing the message: 'To the child of a brave Wigan soldier' (or sailor if applicable) and 'With warmest Christmas greetings from the Mayor's Committee, Christmas 1914'. The chocolate wrapper bore the national colours of the Allies, supporting a portrait of King George on either side, and the right corner bore the borough coat of arms. On

Christmas Eve the children attended distribution points to collect their Yuletide gifts.

The children of the United States of America collected or subscribed to an enormous amount of gifts intended for children whose fathers had been killed in the war. There were so many gifts the fund was extended to include children of those wounded, missing at sea or at the front and also of the Territorials serving in Egypt. The gifts filled the hold of the SS *Jason* known as the Santa Claus ship. Wigan received 633 gifts, mainly woollen garments, but there were other comforts and toys which were distributed from various centres on New Year's Eve. Wigan schoolchildren reciprocated goodwill by sending socks to Alexandria, Egypt for the 5/Manchester Battalion.

On Christmas Eve the wounded men from the Woodlands hospitals were entertained to tea and entertainment at Haigh Hall by the Right Hon. The Earl and Countess of Crawford and Balcarres. On Christmas Day Mr and Mrs Harold Sumner visited the hospitals and presented each man with a khaki holdall containing a knife, fork, spoon, tin-opener and a collapsible aluminium cup. The patients also received postcards from the king and queen, being photographs of their Majesties bearing the words 'With our best wishes for Christmas 1914. May you soon be restored to health'. Mary R. George R.I.

Haigh Hall.

CHAPTER 2

1915
Deepening Conflict

The presentations continued into the New Year with the Wigan and District BRCS distributing Queen Alexandra, the Queen Mother's gift to the hospitalised soldiers. This consisted of a box with a coloured portrait filled with cigarettes each bearing the name 'Alexandra'. The Mayor of Wigan also presented the sick and wounded with an enamel badge and a box of chocolate.

In some sectors of the Western Front chocolate and cigarettes were exchanged during a partial Christmas truce of which first-hand accounts were now appearing in the January press. Londoner Private T. Nash, 1/East Lancashire was a patient at Woodlands Hospital, Wigan suffering from frost-bitten feet and an infected leg caused by being caught in barbed wire:

'On Christmas Day we were in our third month entrenched at a place in Flanders. About 12.00 p.m. the Germans ceased firing, and two or three of them came unarmed out of their trenches and began to walk towards us saying they wished to speak to us. Two or three of our chaps went out to meet them, but an officer called them back suspecting a trap. However, more unarmed Germans came towards us, and then our chaps went out, also unarmed, to meet them, our officer warning them to take every precaution in case of treachery. A few men were left behind in our trenches with their rifles ready to fire if anything happened, but I was among those who went out. There, would be about 400 to 500 Germans and about 200 of us. We all shook hands and fraternized generally, exchanging Christmas greetings, cigarettes, cigars etc., several of the Germans exchanging their watches for our jack-knives. Then our Commanding Officer also came out, and one of the German officers took a photo of us all mixed up together, British and Germans. Our Commanding Officer also arranged a football match between teams of opposing ranks on New Year's Day, but I was relieved from the trenches in the meantime, so I don't know whether it took place or not. We were chatting with them for about two hours, and they told us that they were sorry they were fighting ....'

Private Nash concluded by saying that when they left the trenches to meet the Germans one of their artillery officers went out too, taking notes of the German position from the more advantageous position.

At home, the passing of Christmas and New Year was the signal for renewed activity at recruiting offices. Since the middle of August the Wigan office alone had recruited 4,360 men. Now, in scenes reminiscent of the first waves of patriotism, a steady procession of volunteers marched from the hive of activity that was the Bretherton's Row recruiting offices to the railway station en route to their assigned army depots. The portion of Wallgate between the Market Place and station was lined with the curious, waiting to watch the men depart, and the mothers, wives and families all bidding good luck to their departing loved-ones.

Nationally, thousands of men failed to meet the minimum army height standard; this prompted a Birkenhead MP to request and receive permission to recruit a Bantam battalion raised from men measuring between 5ft and 5ft 3ins tall. At least one would-be Bantam walked all the way from Wigan. Within a few days two battalions of bantams were raised for the Cheshire Regiment. Other towns and cities followed the Birkenhead initiative; suitable Wigan recruits were directed to Bury as on 13 January recruiting commenced for the 18/Lancashire Fusilier Bantam battalion.

Between New Year's Day and 9 January more than 200 men

The Market Hall opened in 1877.

enlisted at Hindley, and at the Ashton-in-Makerfield armoury recruiting office no fewer than 160 men enlisted within three days. Wigan now received permission to form a permanent establishment of two companies of Territorials aged between 19 and 35 years of age as replacement drafts for the Foreign Service battalion. Upwards of 300 men were training in the Drill Hall; they exercised daily in the fields at Swinley and were soon drafted to Southport. Almost 100 recruits had already joined the fledgling Wigan company of the 14th Manchester Regiment, but a further 250 men were required and a recruiting sergeant stayed in Wigan for the sole purpose of raising the men. It was proposed that the company would be captained by the famous Gloucestershire cricketer G.L. Jessop and the NCOs would if possible be Wigan men.

Every available man was required to deliver victory. In the absence of the predicted swift victory, the combatant nations faced a strategic quandary over the most advantageous location to deploy their forces. As a stalemate existed on the Western Front, Germany opted for an overtly defensive strategy in France and Flanders and concentrated on defeating Russia. The respite afforded the beleaguered Allied armies precious time to regroup and absorb inexperienced battalions now arriving from New Zealand, Australia, Canada and the dominions.

In response to civilian disquiet over German naval bombardments,

The Glory of a
Lion is his
Mane.

COPYRIGHT.

The lion's mane is created from the countries of the Empire.

the Royal Navy answered with a victory at the Battle of the Dogger Bank on 24 January. This curtailed the German naval raids, but evidence of poor naval gunnery and ineffectual communications were again ignored.

Three days later two merchant ships were torpedoed without warning by *U20*, in doing so the old fashioned courtesy of preserving life at sea fell by the wayside. Perhaps it was a notification of intent, for on 1 February Germany announced an unrestricted submarine campaign and henceforth ships of any nationality would be sunk without warning. This was soon followed by the German declaration that the waters around the British Isles were a war zone.

On the home front, the difference between life and death was becoming increasingly arbitrary, the latest example of 'Hun frightfulness' occurred on 19 January when Zeppelin airships carried out their first successful bombing raid on Britain. More followed and non-combatant civilians now risked death from air attack and naval bombardment.

Perhaps in the quest for inspiring news the local media were overzealous, for in late January the *Wigan Observer* prematurely announced 'WIGAN HERO WINS VICTORIA CROSS', the suggested recipient being Corporal John Gleaves (26) of 57 Linney Street, off Platt Lane, Wigan. The article stated:

> 'Within a few hours of ushering in the New Year, Gleaves, in spite of a hail of rifle fire and shells ran 130 yards in the very teeth of the enemy fire in order to save the lives of a [wounded] officer and a private of his regiment: a deed so conspicuous in its personal bravery and courage that he is to have bestowed on him the Victoria Cross'.

The stirring deed attracted plaudits from both the council and public, whose appreciation gradually waned, as for reasons unknown Gleaves did not receive Britain's premier gallantry award.

At the battlefront, trenches provided some shelter from the hail of lead and shrapnel in a war where adept use of the spade and pick were as essential as skills at arms. The 31 January *Manchester Courier and Lancashire General Advertiser* reported from Cairo on night operations conducted by one of the Wigan regiments (probably the 5/Manchester):

> Practically all the men are miners, and what they do not know about digging trenches is not worth knowing. The weather was cold and they were waiting in reserve. To keep warm they asked to be allowed to dig themselves in. They worked to such good purpose that when the colonel of the regiment came on the scene a short while after with the brigadier he almost completely walked over his men, who had beaten all records in digging the line. The brigadier's ire when the matter was explained to him turned to joy, and he and his staff prophecy a bad time for the Germans if they ever try to compete with this regiment in sapping and trenching.'

Their esprit de corps differed greatly from the Wigan Volunteer Corps whose 150 members attended a mid-February meeting to decide whether to disband or continue. The bone of contention in Wigan and elsewhere was War Office Regulation 7 under which a man might be called upon at any time to leave his employment and enlist. The indignation faded on hearing the ruling was intended to prevent men of suitable age, and who ought to join the regular forces, using the corps

Greetings from Egypt.

as a screen. There was also resentment against a committee appointed to govern the corps but this was now altered to a committee comprised of officers from the unit. Henceforth the unit would not be exclusive to businessmen, recruits would also be raised from the working class. The reorganisation ensured the continuation of the corps and they decided to apply for affiliation to the Central Association Volunteer Training Corps. The men were obliged to attend forty drills and show a proficiency in musketry practice.

Cap badge of the Wigan Corps of the Lancashire Volunteers.

Motorised versions of the corps were in development. Like many other schemes arising out of the war, the National Motor Volunteers movement was an entirely new formation inaugurated by individual effort and was recognised by the War Office as a centre to organise the motoring public into proficient large mobile units. An important object was to completely organise all private motors and their owners for use in case of invasion or sudden raids by the enemy. The organisation was also suitable for philanthropic work, such as taking convalescing servicemen for health rides, military and quasi-military duties, recruiting, transport of troops etc. A reference to a Wigan and District

National Motor Volunteers unit appeared in the local press on 24 April when a Mr Cooper advised he had entered into a contract for a number of khaki uniforms with which the Wigan members could be supplied at their own expense, the only item the War Office supplied being the GR badge to be worn on the left arm.

The motor cars were supplied by the members at their own expense, they received no Government funding for petrol or vehicle maintenance. The entrance fee was 10s per member, and 1s [5p] a week afterwards towards the expense of the organisation and training. A company was to consist of 100 to 105 cars, each carrying two men, 210 in all. The members were trained by squad drill (about one hour per week), and in military drill and discipline, as untrained motorists were just as unmanageable as untrained infantry. The military training of the men was of the greatest importance. The view of the authorities was that one so trained would be given complete control and any untrained owner or driver could be pressed into service as an orderly.

The drivers would now have to negotiate darkened streets for under Regulation 12 of DORA 1914 air raid precaution lighting restrictions were implemented. The order came into effect on 1 March and applied to the 63rd Regimental District of Manchester, Salford, Ashton-under-Lyne and Wigan borough. The prohibitions included making lighting invisible from above by shading or reducing its intensity; lights on tram cars, railway stations and sidings required reducing to a level sufficient to allow safe conduct of business; all outside advertising signs to be extinguished; in brightly lit streets a portion of lights had to be extinguished to break up rows of lights; intensely lit shop fronts and motor car headlights were prohibited. The Wigan borough black-out was officially rescinded in mid-April.

But the risk of attack by raid, bombardment or aircraft prompted the Mayor of Wigan, in conjunction with the Military and Civil Authorities, to issue a 15 February instruction to the press. In the event of an attack, all civilians were to remain indoors or return home, non-combatants were not allowed on the streets. Inhabitants were instructed to shelter in cellars until the danger passed. Surgeons and doctors were required to remain at their surgeries or houses until they received instructions from the authorities.

As battle casualties increased, indignation aimed at the 'stay at homes' intensified. The male munition workers were not discernible from men avoiding military service; these together with 'slackers or shirkers', were scorned at every opportunity. Incensed women would present a white feather or shower the stay-at-home in white chicken feathers. To prevent the social castigation of those 'doing their bit', in March the Government issued a 45mm high oval brass lapel badge for male Ministry of Munitions workers employed in 'starred' or 'certified' production of 'any commodity directly required for the fulfilment of any contract with the Ministry of Munitions, the War Office or the Admiralty'.

Male munitions worker's badge.

Manufacturing problems were aggravated by high absenteeism mainly due to alcoholic remorse. Prohibiting the sale of alcohol would have proven controversial and costly in taxation, but excessive consumption of alcohol was proving detrimental to industrial output. Public house opening hours were reduced by military order accordingly: licensed houses could only open from 10am to 10pm on weekdays, the Sunday opening hours being 12.30pm to 2.30pm and 6.30 to 9pm. On the recommendation of the Chief Constable of Wigan, the Secretary of State approved an order for public houses and clubs to close at 9.30pm on weekdays and 8.30pm on Sundays. The approval was received on 3 April and the unpopular order took effect from that day. A June attempt to increase licensing hours in line with other towns where the order existed was refused by Wigan magistrates.

The town bustled with martial comings and goings including 1,400 Bantams of the 18/Lancashire Fusiliers who, on 8 April, took up residence at Garswood Park, Ashton-in-Makerfield. They became regular visitors to the Ashton YMCA that offered refreshments, two billiard tables, board games, letter writing and a home from home atmosphere.

On Saturday 18 April a four-day recruiting campaign saw Wigan take on the appearance of a barrack town. 'At all points the martial blare of bugles and rolls of drums could be heard, while the ordered tread of well drilled feet was accompanied by the stirring music of a well drilled band'. The object was to attract 160 recruits for the Wigan Pals company undergoing training at Lichfield. A detachment of the pals, comprising forty drummers and buglers and forty other ranks arrived at the North West Railway station at midday. Crowds lined the route from the station to the drill hall where the men were quartered. After lunch they marched through the town, joined by the Wigan Volunteer Corps and others. Tea and more marching followed, then the men were dismissed for recruiting purposes. The Sabbath was spent largely in church parades.

The biggest day in the campaign was Monday. The first parade was 9.30am followed by a march to Hindley, returning through Lower Ince to Wigan drill hall for dinner. At 2pm, they marched to the London and North Western (L&NW) station in Wigan and met the Liverpool Pals band. The 200-strong procession proceeded around Poolstock and back up Wallgate to Rowbottom Square where they were dismissed. By the next day sixty-two pals had enlisted and a further 120 recruits volunteered for other units.

A fortnight earlier a Schools Training Corps was inaugurated in Wigan for the purpose of imparting physical and military drill to youths aged between fifteen and eighteen years of age in preparation for military service.

The home front infrastructure may have been progressing nicely but British industry responded lethargically to the clamour for artillery shells. Following *The Times* reporting of the Neuve Chapelle shell shortage, the pressure applied by the Conservative Party brought about the collapse of the Liberal Government. The new coalition government established a Ministry of Munitions under the auspices of David Lloyd George. On 21 April he stated:

The Roll of Honour

IS YOUR NAME on a ROLL of HONOUR ?

IF YOUR NAME goes down on your firm's Roll of Honour, it also goes on that mighty Scroll which records the names of all who have rallied round the Flag.

There is room for your name on the Roll of Honour.

Ask your employer to keep your position open for you. Tell him that you are going to the help of the Empire. Every patriotic employer is assisting his men to enlist, and he'll do the right thing by you.

Tell him NOW—

Your King and Country Want you——TO-DAY.

At any Post Office you can obtain the address of the nearest Recruiting Officer.

GOD SAVE THE KING.

A 'soldier of the king' advert.

'During the fortnight of fighting in and around Neuve Chapelle almost as much ammunition was spent by our artillery as during the whole of the two and three quarter years of the Boer War. The urgent need for the country, then, is for shells, shells and more shells. . . A radical change of organization is necessary and it must be carried out at once.'

He was also a long term supporter of the Temperance movement; in March 1915 he famously stated: 'We are fighting Germans, Austrians and Drink, and as far as I can see the greatest of these foes is Drink.' He also persuaded George V to lead by example and pledge that the

David Lloyd George.

royal household would abstain from alcohol for the duration of the war.

The shorter drinking hours may have been financially beneficial to those affected by the high and rapidly advancing prices of coal, meat, bread, flour (now double the August price) and other necessities. Inflation pressed particularly heavily on those whose life was already a struggle for bare subsistence. Across the country, trade unions campaigned for increased pay in the form of a war bonus. Locally, on behalf of the region's 30,000 members of the allied engineering trades, the union negotiated a settlement with the Board of Trade, which agreed that the wages of the trade union members concerned should be advanced 3s. The announcement on 27 April regarded the payment as necessary due to and dependent on the existence of the abnormal conditions now prevailing in consequence of the war.

Despite inflation, vigorous community fundraising continued. The members of the Parbold VAD (EL 50), unable to join the several members on duty in various hospitals, arranged a late April jumble sale supported by the tea making ladies of the Parbold Knitting Party. The sale generated £74 for the Wigan and District Red Cross Division. Since the start of the war the Parbold Knitting Party, together with working parties at Dalton and Newburgh, had contributed 1,450 comforts for soldiers and sailors. Several days later, the recently formed Ince branch of the British Red Cross Society held a successful fund raising American Tea in the public hall.

Meanwhile the Corporation Industries Committee attempted to attract new manufacturers to Wigan, particularly those capitalising on the manufacture of goods and materials previously sourced from Germany. Amongst the Wigan manufacturers awarded War Office contracts was a large clothing firm (presumably Coops), whose factory and every out-worker's premises were regularly inspected. Health officials found five of the workers had scarlet fever, and as a safeguard on 27 February, the War Office ordered the disinfection of all the premises and clothing; over 1,000 tins of disinfectant were used.

As the borough health workers strove to contain infectious diseases, the Western Front continued to consume a generation. In an attempt to break the siege warfare deadlock, Britain controversially launched an Anglo-French campaign against the Turkish army at Gallipoli. Anglo-French warships attempted to force the Dardanelles Strait to open up the supply route to Russia's Black Sea ports, but they suffered a humiliating defeat.

On 25 April, the Allies made amphibious landings on the Gallipoli Peninsula. The 1st Lancashire Fusiliers, a component of 29th Division's 86 Brigade, were ordered to land on the 300-yard wide W Beach (later known as Lancashire Landing) then attack Hills 114 and 138. The Royal Fusiliers would strike inland from X Beach and other 29th Division units from the easterly V Beach would link and make a united advance on the Turkish positions. Minutes before the first Lancashire Fusilier rowing boats grounded on W Beach, the Turks fired a maelstrom of lead into the crammed cutters. Led by their officers, the ambushed 1/Lancashire Fusiliers struggled ashore bedevilled by small-arms fire, the depth of water, submerged barbed wire and their weighty equipment. The slopes and the summit of the cliffs had been entrenched, and a low ridge overlooking the centre of the beach was commanded by two heavily wired redoubts on the high ground above the cliffs, at a distance of 600 yards. The beach itself was a 'death trap'.

Major General Sir Aylmer Hunter-Weston, the officer commanding 29th Division, described the landing as 'a deed of heroism that has seldom been equalled' and recommended the bestowal of six Victoria Crosses on the two most distinguished officers and the four most distinguished NCOs and men. The 24 August *London Gazette*

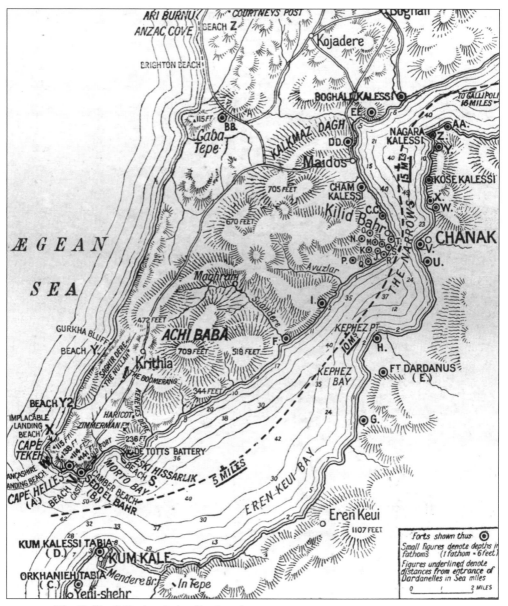

The Gallipoli Peninsula landing beaches.

announced the awarding of the Victoria Cross to the following Lancashire Fusiliers: Captain Richard Raymond Willis, Sergeant Alfred Joseph Richards and Private William Keneally, who shared the following citation:

'On 25 April 1915 west of Cape Helles, Gallipoli, three companies and the Headquarters of the 1st Lancashire Fusiliers, when landing on W Beach, were met by a deadly fire from hidden machine-guns which caused a large number of casualties. The survivors, however, rushed up and cut wire entanglements notwithstanding the terrific fire from the enemy and, after overcoming supreme difficulties, the cliffs were gained and the position maintained.'

Private William Keneally VC.

Private William Keneally VC was the son of Colour Sergeant John Stephen Keneally who had served twenty-four years in the Royal Irish Regiment and had four others sons in the Army. William, who was 25-years-old, was in India for six of the seven years of his first period in the Army. He then worked as a miner at Low Green Colliery, Wigan and enlisted on the outbreak of war. The confirmation of the award came too late, for the hero was seriously wounded and reported missing in the 28 June Battle of Gully Ravine.

Three other recommendations were not expediently processed, but Corporal John Elisha Grimshaw, who was born in Abram, Wigan was awarded the Distinguished Conduct Medal, upgraded in March 1917 to the Victoria Cross.

Sergeant Alfred Joseph Richards VC.

Meanwhile on the Western Front, near Ypres on 22 April the Germans had deployed their latest example of hideousness – poison gas; but their heinous attempt to break the deadlock failed. Throughout the year the British attempted to wrest insignificant villages from the German invader and the life sapping battlefields of Loos, Neuve Chapelle and the Ypres salient rapidly attained their own notoriety to the war weary soldiers of 1915.

Every eligible man was needed at the front, a late April Wigan Civilian Recruiting Committee campaign concluded with an evening meeting held in the Assembly Room of the Wigan Mining College. A circular advertising the meeting stated:

Wigan Mining and Technical College.

'Dear Friend. Football matches, horseracing, evening entertainments go on as usual. You get breakfast, dinner, tea, supper as usual. You are led to think "How does this war concern me?" If ever the Germans break through the ring of our Grand Fleet you'll soon jolly well find out, Wigan laid in ruins, you and your mankind shot down without pity, your women-folk and sweethearts treated in such a way that death would be preferable.

Ask yourself these questions. 1. Is it essential to the welfare of Wigan and district that I should stop here at my present job? 2. Am I really necessary at home? 3. Am I doing anything except wearing a patriotic badge to help my country and my brave fellow-townsmen who are fighting in the trenches? 4. Have I a weak heart or a lame leg?

If you feel a bit bothered and uncertain in your mind, attend the great meeting announced on the other side and swell the ranks of the thousands of brave men who are still coming forward in the defence of our country.'

Worse was to come: the war at sea plumbed new depths on 7 May when the Liverpool bound Cunard vessel RMS *Lusitania* was steaming 15 miles off the Irish coast. A torpedo from the German submarine *U20* struck the transatlantic liner, she sank in minutes and 1,198 souls perished, including 124 American citizens. Among the second-class passengers on the ill-fated *Lusitania* were Mr and Mrs Edward Lawrenson who had left Wigan twenty-eight years previously to live in Michel, British Columbia where Mr Lawrenson was involved in the mining industry. Having made good, 58-year-old Mr Lawrenson decided to bring his wife Elizabeth home to Wigan. A fortnight prior to sailing Elizabeth wrote to her sister, Mrs Richard Davies, Gibraltar Hotel, Scholes advising they were sailing on the *Lusitania*; it was the last news of them.

The 'cold blooded outrage' fuelled anti-German riots in London, Liverpool and Manchester. The day after the sinking there was a Wigan demonstration against one tradesman, and had it not been for the activity of the police, damage to property and personal injury may have ensued. On 10 May, the Wigan Civilian Recruiting Committee (with an eye to the main chance) arranged a public meeting in Wigan Market Square. Hundreds of incensed residents attended, and the following message was forwarded to the Prime Minister:

> 'That this meeting of Wigan folk expresses its profound sympathy with those who mourn for relatives and friends lost in the *Lusitania* and its indignation at the devilish action of the Germans in sinking that ship and pledges itself to obtain all the men possible to enable Sir John Jellicoe and Sir John French to crush the hoards of German murderers.'

The German use of poisonous gas and the *Lusitania* death toll intensified ill feeling against aliens. In mid-May the Chief Constable of Wigan took steps to remove the following five un-naturalised Germans and Austrians of military age to the Lancaster internment camp.

German born Ernest T. Muller (35) had served in the Jaeger Infantry. He was an engineering designer at Walkers Foundry but left days earlier due to his work mates' murmurings. Threatening letters were delivered to his Hodges Street home and he feared for the safety

A
German Naval Victory

"With joyful pride we contemplate this latest deed of our navy. . . .
Kölnische Volkszeitung, 10th May, 1915.

This medal has been struck in Germany with the object of keeping alive in German hearts the recollection of the glorious achievement of the German Navy in deliberately destroying an unarmed passenger ship, together with 1,198 non-combatants, men, women and children.

On the obverse, under the legend "No contraband" *(Keine Bannware),* there is a representation of the *Lusitania* sinking. The designer has put in guns and aeroplanes, which (as was certified by United States Government officials after inspection) the *Lusitania* did *not* carry ; but has conveniently omitted to put in the women and children, which the world knows she *did* carry.

On the reverse, under the legend "Business above all" *(Geschäft über alles),* the figure of Death sits at the booking office of the Cunard Line and gives out tickets to passengers, who refuse to attend to the warning against submarines given by a German. This picture seeks apparently to propound the theory that if a murderer warns his victim of his intention, the guilt of the crime will rest with the victim, not with the murderer.

The Lusitania *medallion.*

of his wife and young child. The family intended moving to America but he was arrested before the Secretary of State granted emigration permission.

George Pietsch (52) was born in Germany and was three years within the military age. He resided in Hallgate and was a butcher by trade.

The previously mentioned George Brand (42) was formerly a Co-op butcher who had previously been detained and released, but was then unable to gain employment. He had resided in Wigan for a number

GERMAN PRISONERS IN A BARBED WIRE COMPOUND
WHERE MOST OF THE GERMANS IN THIS COUNTRY OUGHT TO BE. ::

Interned German prisoners.

of years and had the support of many people but became a victim of circumstances.

Carl Abetill (52) was born in Austria and had lived in this country for thirty years. He was employed by Livesey of Queen Street. An expert carver of wood and stone, one of his sculptures occupied a prominent position in Bolton.

Claud Harry Blanken (44) was born 8 May 1871, his mother went to Germany for the birth and returned days later.

The five were arrested, paraded at the police station and taken to the station in two cars where the husbands stoically bid farewell to their families.

The intolerance of foreigners did not extend to our Allies, in mid-May Wigan being one of the first towns to hold a Russian Flag Day to alleviate the sufferings of Russian and British wounded. Stalls throughout the town sold 50,000 neat little white flags with a blue cross and collected over £200. The efforts of school teachers, their pupils, boy scouts and other workers were praised.

Also impressed was Mr Valentine Williams who wrote home concerning the toil of the sapper, his arduous conditions of work and the perils of his calling in comparison to the five-days-a-week factory slackers. His letter forwarded from the British Headquarters in France appeared in a late May edition of the *Standard*:

> 'I went down a mine. . .You entered it by a shaft supported by baulks of timber. A greasy knotted rope was the means of descent, and guttering candles, stuck on the baulks by their own grease, provided the illumination.

Sounds of a hot altercation floated up the shaft as I gripped the rope to descend. At the foot of the shaft a cheerful person, smeared from head to foot with yellow clay, was gently chaffing a Lancashire voice emerging from the entrance to a low gallery running out at right angles to the shaft. The owner of the voice appeared. He was a thick set, well developed man, the typical North-country miner, clad in a sleeveless singlet open at the chest and trousers thrust into trench boots. He was daubed all over with the yellow clay. It was in his hair, and round his eyes, and all over his brawny arms.

He was carrying on a lurid conversation with his mate regarding the perverse inclination of the clay to stick to him. He was not disposed for conversation. I asked where he came from, 'Fra Wigan'! he said, wiping the dirt from his eyes, and disappearing down the gallery – Wigan in Flanders.

> I followed him down the mine. Imagine a low gallery along which you can only advance doubled up, with a plank flooring ankle deep in mud and water, a chill damp air, and water dripping constantly. . .Where the mine ended stood another man 'Fra Wigan', in singlet and trousers bent double hacking away with pick and shovel at the wall of clay in front of them. Two miners doing their bit for England. . .'

At the beginning of June, Liverpool, Manchester and Blackburn were chosen as the centres for organising munitions in the North and North-east Lancashire district. Members of the Munitions Organising Committee for Blackburn, to which Wigan was associated, visited the borough to ascertain what works were suitable for the manufacture of munitions etc.

Later in the month, due to Wigan and district companies being largely engaged on various Army contracts for motor wagons, khaki, shell and explosives, the Mayor of Wigan placed the old council chamber at the disposal of the Munitions Works Bureau. Along with other duties, the bureau now conducted a labour recruitment drive which involved opening for two hours on weekday evenings and weekend afternoons. Engineering workers not already engaged on munitions work, were invited to sign on for six months work and agree to be transferred to any place involved in munitions work; there was no shortage of highly skilled applicants.

Other men from the district served in the 42nd (East Lancashire) Division which had landed at Gallipoli on 6 May, and took part in the 4 June Third Battle of Krithia. The 23 June edition of the *Liverpool Echo* reported the Wigan losses of the 5/Manchester comprised fourteen killed, four died of wounds, one dangerously ill, two ill and 102 wounded. Included among the wounded were Lieutenant Basil L. Fletcher, Lieutenant P.C. Fletcher, Second Lieutenant M.K. Burrows and Second Lieutenant Eric J. Burrows. The first two were sons of Colonel Fletcher, the third was the son of Mr J.S. Burrows, the three parents being owners of Fletcher Burrows and Company, a Lancashire colliery. Bedevilled from the outset by inept leadership, the campaign ultimately became a military fiasco.

Globally, the heavy casualties fuelled the need for even more recruits. The Territorial Force raised second and third line units leading to the Manchester Regiment having vacancies for 6,000 men including 769 men required for the 3/5 Manchester formed on 5 May and based at Wigan Drill Hall. The alarming casualty levels were counter-productive to voluntarism. For example during eleven months of warfare 90,000 men from the Manchester district had rallied to the flag but numbers were in sharp decline. On 2 July only forty-five Manchester and district recruits enlisted, raising speculation the week's returns would be the lowest since the war started. Due to waning national recruitment, the government appointed Lord Derby to implement a system of compulsory military service. The first steps towards conscription involved a national canvas to ascertain how many eligible men were in war service occupations or were avoiding military service. The first targets of the Derby Scheme were single men with no dependents.

Under the National Registration Act, Wigan Corporation was

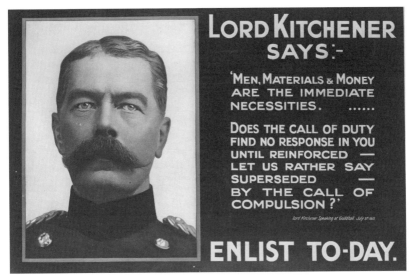

A blunt extract from a speech by Lord Kitchener.

required to compile and maintain a section of the National Register. Similar to a census, the forms would be left at each house to be completed by every inhabitant between the ages of fifteen and sixty-five on 15 August; the Town Clerk estimated the borough had approximately 58,500 houses. As a preliminary the Town Clerk wrote to the heads of the Corporation departments and the heads of Wigan schools requesting voluntary enumerators for compiling the register; with few exceptions they agreed to distribute and collect the registration forms. The work of enumeration would commence on Monday 9 August and finish on the 14th, the enumerators would return to collect the forms on 16, 17, and 18 August.

And on 12 July town councillors were read a letter from Magee Marshall Ltd, stating that in consequence of German hostility of local people against the name of Von Blücher Square, they had irregularly altered the name to Alexandra Square and requested the council to formalise the name change. Accordingly the Town Clerk was instructed to take the necessary steps to adopt the new name and charge any incidental expense to the company. The adjoining Von Blücher public house faced the merged Lindsay and Alexandra pits, the hostelry also cast aside its Germanic name and became The Alexandra. In doing so a century old acknowledgement to the Prussian Field Marshall Gebhard Leberecht von Blücher, ally of the Duke of Wellington, who defeated Napoleon I a century earlier at Waterloo, was airbrushed from history.

Some time had elapsed since the announcement that the country was organising its resources with a view to securing the maximum output of war munitions. Locally it was felt Wigan was somewhat late in making a show. The Blackburn committee was invited to ascertain whether firms in the Wigan district could produce shells or manufacture certain components. The committee had power to make preliminary arrangements prior to the Ministry of Munitions entering into contracts. Interested contractors could see examples of shells and other devices displayed in the Town Clerk's office. The shells urgently required were 3.3ins (18-pounder), 4.5ins and 6ins high explosives.

Also in late July, the Garswood Manufacturing Company offered the committee the use of their weaving shed as a munitions factory. A month later the Northern Coarse Spinners announced they had secured a town centre plot of land for an extensive single storey building lit with electricity. This new industry to the town would spin cotton waste, a trade previously largely controlled by Germany.

The 1 July establishment of the Ministry of Munitions, managed by David Lloyd George, impacted severely on working life. Under the Munitions of War Act workers were required to be diligent in attendance and work to full efficiency, failure to do so would inevitably lead to the offender appearing before a tribunal. The tribunals met throughout the war and some of the local misdemeanours included the mid July appearance of Thomas Jones, a furnace man at Church Ironworks, Ince. The defendant should have been at work in order to have the furnace ready for rollers early in the morning. He failed to do so and forty men were left without employment. The defendant admitted his guilt, and said he had been drinking with soldiers. He was fined 20s for wrongfully leaving his munitions employment.

Under the Munitions of War Act, known in some regions as the 'Slavery Act', one of the restrictions prevented workmen leaving their place of employment to go elsewhere. At Wigan, five fitters and colliers employed by the Pemberton Colliery Company were summonsed for

How I felt before the tribunal.

absenteeism from work without notice. Two of the fitters in the coal-getting and coal-screening department left in July without giving fourteen days notice. They went to work at Cammell Laird in Birkenhead where they earned as much as £3 (60s) a week instead of the 38s at the colliery. The prosecution proved that during their unauthorised absence other fitters had to work overtime on important jobs and the damage claimed was £1 and 19s respectively. The defendants were ordered to pay the damages and 10s costs.

Patrick McAvoy, a collier who had lost seventy-five per cent of his time, leading to the loss of 40.5 tons of coal amounting to £5 19s 3d, gave the excuse he had been entertaining friends in Scotland. He was ordered to pay the damages and 20s costs.

Isaac Middlehurst was a fireman from whom £2 2s 2d was claimed admitted being off work due to meeting and drinking with friends. He was ordered to pay the damage and 10s costs.

Less self-centred individuals, included three wounded soldiers from the Woodlands who participated in yet another fund raising 'French Flag Day'. In late July, 100,000 miniature emblems of the French flag were distributed throughout Wigan and district. The lapel flags were priced at 1d, 6d and 1s and some 80,000 penny flags were sold in Wigan. The flag-day raised £381 for wounded servicemen.

By the first anniversary of the war rising food prices and house rent fuelled industrial unrest. As the bank holiday approached the Wigan Corporation tramway manager received a letter stating that the motormen, conductors and others wanted a 1/2d an hour pay increase and 1d for all electricians employed.

Tram No.12, a Dick Kerr open top, passing the Plantation Gates entrance to Haigh Hall.

Although the union advised against the stoppage, on 3 August the men went on strike. Some 37 miles of track fell idle and an estimated 1,500 miners were unable to get to work. There was an absence of public sympathy as the men who were mainly holding temporary positions were considered well paid and taking advantage of the situation when fifty-three tramway men were with the colours. The next day the dispute was referred to the War Productions Committee and the tram service resumed. Weeks later the arbitration committee awarded a wages increase of one farthing (1/4d) an hour for conductors; the other wages remained unaltered.

The National Registration enumerator's work commenced on 9 August; penalties were imposed on anyone who refused to or neglected to complete the forms. When the register was compiled it fell to the

National Registration.

Corporation to issue every registered person a certificate. Maintaining the register was also the Corporation's responsibility, and on 6 October it was agreed to pay 15s a week for a vacant room on the ground floor of the temporary municipal offices in King Street West.

Following the cessation of German imports Wigan councillors attempted to exploit the ban on German imports, in particular the aniline dye industry of which Germany had a world monopoly, only ten per cent of the dyestuffs consumed in the country being manufactured by British firms. The plant involved in dye production produced various by products used in the chemical industry. In February a councillor suggested that, with the co-operation of the Gas Works, they would be able to produce benzene, anthracene, toluol [toluene] and carbolic acid. This might encourage manufacturers to establish a branch of the aniline dye industry.

As part of a national drive to produce large quantities of artillery explosives, on 14 August the manager of Wigan Corporation Gas Works advised the Council Gas Committee of measures taken to increase the amount of toluene contained in the saleable commodity known as gas tar, essentially a by-product of coal-gas production. Gas tar provided the prime source of toluene, which is the base of tri-nitro-toluol (TNT) the high explosive used in shells. The Government requested gas companies to adopt certain processes known for increasing the quantity of toluene in the tar. At modest cost, the Wigan works adapted part of their plant and tests at Manchester University showed the quantity of toluene in the tar had doubled: 200 gallons of tar before treatment contained 1.28 gallons of toluene, and after treatment 2.56 gallons. As toluene was a national necessity, the Wigan Corporation gas works manager hoped to receive 1/6d per ton extra.

The cry of 'We want more' echoed throughout the nation. At the beginning of August a strong patriotic appeal was made to the young men of Ashton-in-Makerfield where two open air meetings were held, the first at Rose Hill and the second near the Record Mill in Princess Street. At the first meeting the Reverend A. White, who presided, urged men to join the 5/South Lancashire. A wounded officer declared: 'The man who would not fight for England had no right to be in England'.

At the second meeting Mary, Lady Gerard implored mothers with eligible sons to let them go to the front. It was hard, as she herself knew as her only son had gone and was severely wounded (shot through the shoulder, the bullet passed down his back and grazed his lung), and was for three weeks in danger of losing his life. He had recovered, returned to the front, and had since been sent home on military duties. She would have been ashamed if her son had not joined the forces. Councillor Walden mentioned that in that very street there were families with several sons who had sent nobody to the front, in contrast to their neighbours' absent sons and fathers. The announcement that Ashton had sent almost 1,200 men to the Army and that 550 of them were married was greeted with loud applause.

Also looking for endorsement were 29th Division officers seeking Victoria Cross recommendations for three of the Lancashire Landing fusiliers in compliance with Rule 13. This permitted a commanding officer of equally brave men to conduct a ballot among those involved in a gallant act of daring performed by no less than fifty men. As a result on 15 March 1917 the *London Gazette* announced the bestowal of Victoria Crosses to Major Cuthbert Bromley, Corporal John Elisha Grimshaw and Sergeant Frank Edward Stubbs. The heroes shared the identical Lancashire Landing citation as the other recipients.

The wounded were also treated as heroes, including four Wigan men serving with 5/Manchester who arrived at the Royal Albert Infirmary in mid August. The hospital provided fifty beds for soldiers. The hospital acting general secretary reported that a ward was set aside for operative cases, in which men eligible for the Army but not

Three Lancashire Fusilier VC recipients.

| CORP. (NOW SERGT.) GRIMSHAW, Lancashire Fusiliers. | SERGT. F. E. STUBBS, Lancashire Fusiliers. | CAPT. (TEMP. MAJOR) BROMLEY, C.B., Lancashire Fusiliers. |

physically fit, underwent operations to make them fit for front line duty. Up to March no fewer than 105 had passed through the ward, and since then numbers had proportionately increased, which proved Wigan lads were undaunted by what may have happened to their friends and were prepared to take their chances against the formidable German forces. This was seen as a remarkable example of pluck and should impel physically fit shirkers to think seriously about what they should be doing.

As did General MacKinnon, the Commander in Chief of the Western Command, who notified the Wigan Chief Constable under Regulation 10 of DORA that with effect from 28 August all licensed premises were closed for the sale, supply and consumption of intoxicating liquor to any NCO or soldiers who were patients of any military hospital or auxiliary hospital in Western Command.

At the beginning of September the divisional Inspector of Mines reported that the output of coal had reduced since the war began, contributory factors being absenteeism and the depletion of experienced miners due to Army recruitment and the introduction of

The bottom of a coal pit shaft.

inexperienced workers. Except for the undesirable reduction of our coal supply it would be highly satisfactory to record eighty-five per cent of the miners of military age in St Helens, Wigan and Manchester districts had enlisted. The AGM of the Pearson and Knowles Coal and Iron Company Ltd reported that 3,100 employees had joined the forces, including Moss Hall worker William Keneally VC, but despite the depleted workforce the company would continue to provide the necessary munitions to prosecute the war.

The insatiable demand for more recruits involved an autumn recruitment drive for 10,000 men to fill up the reserve companies of the East Lancashire Division fighting at Gallipoli. Amongst them were Sub Lieutenant S.H. Fish, and Sub Lieutenant J. Curzon Hilton who wrote home:

'It may interest you to know what a familiar object a Deakin's jam tin is out here in Gallipoli. As Wiganers, we were very pleased to see 'Deakin's – Wigan' on tins of what forms a large portion of our diet, and when we found our battalion stores was largely built of Deakin's boxes, we felt quite at home. But the ultimate end of the empty tins is the most interesting thing, for they are made into bombs to hurl at the Turks, and have done yeoman service as hand grenades. Yesterday we were watching our bombs at work with a catapult, and they made some excellent practice at the Turkish trenches some 150 yards away with these bombs.'

The above Deakin's boxes were sturdy War Office Export crates. The jam factory at the Eclipse Works, Bradford Place, Wigan, had received a War Office contract for over 300 tons of jam comprising 100,000 tins, each containing 1lb of jam to be delivered by the end of 1914; evidently part of the consignment reached Gallipoli.

Also expecting delivery were the choirs and Sunday schools of the Wigan Rural Deanery who had forsaken their day trips and raised £500 for an ambulance. In August Canon Mathews forwarded the donation to the Joint War Committee who advised that the vehicle would go to the front as soon as possible. On 2 October, about 7,000 people gathered at Wigan to witness Dr Chavasse, the Bishop of Liverpool, dedicate the ambulance. His Lordship said, 'the mothers and fathers of

Bystander copyright.

THE ETERNAL QUESTION
" When the 'ell is it goin' to be strawberry ? "

the land had shown their self-sacrifice by giving their best and dearest'.

The bishop would ultimately lose his own son, Captain Noel Chavasse, who was twice awarded the Victoria Cross (VC and Bar) as well as the Military Cross for his 'courage and self-sacrifice. . . beyond praise' serving as a doctor with the Royal Army Medical Corps. Several days after the dedication, the vicar of Haigh Parish Church, the Reverend C.H. James received news that his eldest son, Corporal Charles Edward James (31), 13/Middlesex, had been reported missing in France (killed 26 September). The vicar had previously had two sons killed in the Dardanelles – Lieutenant F.A. James and Lieutenant Sydney James of 5/Manchester.

At home, the first anniversary of the opening of Woodlands No.1 was celebrated with a fete on 6 October. Friends of hospital staff visited and brought gifts in money or kind to the value or weight of a pound to augment the hospital stores. During the afternoon representatives of the Hippodrome gave a concert under the direction of Mr Clair, who also gave the wounded cigarettes from his cigarette fund. Fundraising for additional surgical and pharmaceutical appliances for use in the Red Cross Hospitals of the Wigan and District Division almost doubled the £50 target.

A week later, on 13 October the Garswood Hall Red Cross Hospital also held a 'Pound Day' to mark twelve months' completion of voluntary treatment of the wounded. Visitors arrived from 2pm bearing gifts of tea, coffee, rice, bread, tinned food, fruit, meat, towels, antiseptic, soaps and wadding and the all important cash donations. The day proved a great success. The hospital had recently added a third ward, raising the accommodation to thirty-eight beds. The wards were situated in the Dining Room (Number 1 Ward), Ball Room (Number 2 Ward) and an anteroom of the Drawing Room (Number 3 Ward). The latter room had six beds provided by the local Red Cross Commandant Mary, Lady Gerard who also covered the heating and lighting expenses. Other rooms in the hall served as a soldiers' smoke room, an operating theatre, offices and stores. The extensive grounds proved ample space for recreation for the convalescents.

Overseas soldiers were in less salubrious surroundings. A native of Wigan, Driver J. Clayton (74640) C Battery, 124 Brigade, 37th Division wrote from 'somewhere in France':

'Practically all our battery consists of Wiganers; in fact there are a number of Wiganers in every battery of the brigade. It is now about 8pm, and we are just going to get down for a night's sleep in an old barn where we are billeted which we have christened the Pavilion. But do not think they show pictures in it because of its name. Near our billet is a large wood where our horses are picketed, and in our leisure moments, which are very few, we make a ball out of a sack and have a game of rugby. It would do good to see us showing the cockneys how to play it; they think they are playing soccer.

The Germans are at present very quiet, but we must not think they are beaten, as they are a long way from it. We think it will take all our men to do this and a few more if we can get hold of them. According to what we hear there are a few slackers walking around King Street, who are fit for service. We think it would be a bit more honour for them to enlist rather than parade the streets.

P.S. We would be grateful if somebody would send an old rugby ball so we can keep ourselves warm this winter and have an enjoyable time.'

Perhaps the Wigan Service League forwarded the requested ball, for as October drew to a close, they received permission from the War Office to be a recognised organisation for the sending of parcels free of charge to the troops in France, Belgium, the Dardanelles and prisoners of war. When the scheme started, parcels were received at 4 Woodcock Street, Wigan. Each bore the full details of the serviceman and battalion or unit and contained a list of the contents – no matches were allowed. When sufficient parcels had accumulated for any unit, they were forwarded to the commanding officer of the unit through the military forwarding officer. Parcels forwarded to prisoners of war could not contain tinned goods as the tin could be re-cycled by the Germans.

Weekly concerts raised funds for prisoner of war comforts. Of the many examples reported, by October the Parbold Work Room had made and despatched some 4,500 comfort articles. An Orrell concert held in late November raised £13-12s-2d, partly spent on the provision of warm woollen pants, shirts, vests and rugs for the prisoners at Sennelager Camp, Germany. The parcels may have been forwarded through the recently opened parcel receiving rooms in Tower Buildings, Wallgate, Wigan.

The town had its fair share of army defaulters, including James Monks who deserted from the South Lancashire Regiment which led to police visiting the Golbourne home of Ann Harrison. After denying sheltering a deserter, the police were invited to search her home, they noticed a ceiling attic access was open and Monks was discovered in the attic and arrested. The bench dealt leniently with the prisoner as it was the first case of the kind they had had, but warned subsequent offences would face up to six months imprisonment. The soldier was remanded and taken under escort to his regiment; Mrs Harrison received fourteen days hard labour.

Unmarried.		Married.	
Age.	Group.	Age.	Group.
18–19[1]	1	18–19[1]	24
19–20	2	19–20	25
20–21	3	20–21	26
21–22	4	21–22	27
22–23	5	22–23	28
23–24	6	23–24	29
24–25	7	24–25	30
25–26	8	25–26	31
26–27	9	26–27	32
27–28	10	27–28	33
28–29	11	28–29	34
29–30	12	29–30	35
30–31	13	30–31	36
31–32	14	31–32	37
32–33	15	32–33	38
33–34	16	33–34	39
34–35	17	34–35	40
35–36	18	35–36	41
36–37	19	36–37	42
37–38	20	37–38	43
38–39	21	38–39	44
39–40	22	39–40	45
40–41	23	40–41	46

The Group Scheme: a bureaucratic nightmare of forty-six categories of men.

Society frowned on anything detrimental to the call to arms. On 11 October Lord Derby was appointed Director General and several days later launched the Group Scheme; it was unofficially known as the Derby Scheme, which aimed to induce men between the ages of 18 and 40 to attest their willingness to serve. On doing so, they received armlets bearing the Royal Crown signifying that they were waiting their turn to be called up if required. The scheme was divided into forty-six groups; no man in these groups would be called up until he had reached 19 years of age, and single men would be called up first. The last day to join the scheme was originally 15 December 1915.

Recruitment and high industrial output were the essentials for victory and to this end the Government took control of some companies producing the wide-ranging category of munitions. During November a portion of the ironworks and all of the steel works of the Wigan Coal and Iron Company, Kirkless came under Government control.

From Saturday, 4 December the 'ancient and loyal borough' experienced an upsurge in recruitment due to men intent on pre-empting the 11 December voluntary enlistment deadline. Recruiting stations were overwhelmed, Wigan staff numbers were increased and within a few days a second large office was utilised. For several frenetic days from the early hours until late at night, Wigan and district recruits queued stoically along Bretherton's Row and Wallgate. Such was the pressure on recruitment that the Group System deadline was extended to 15 December, although enlistment directly into both Regular units and the Territorial Force continued.

Two members of the RAMC, Privates Harry Holland of 162 Old Road, Ashton and William Williams of 187 Central Terrace, Clipley Lane, Haydock were stationed at 1st Western General Hospital, Fazakerley. On Saturday, 4 December they were returning by train from weekend leave when a fatal explosion occurred. Various newspaper accounts described the explosive device as a fuse, bomb, grenade, or nose cap off a German shell; the *Wigan Examiner* opted for a fatal bomb explosion.

Williams boarded the 9.20pm train at St Helens, changed trains at Rainford Junction for Fazakerley and entered a compartment solely occupied by Holland. As the train neared Kirby, Holland, who had a brother at the front, took from his greatcoat a time grenade which his

It will be a sad day for the bally German when my group is called up

Germans beware.

brother had brought home on leave, and placed it in William's hand for examination.

> '…before many seconds were over the grenade, which had probably been timed by Holland extracting it from his pocket, exploded with terrific force. William's hand on which the grenade rested was blown completely off, and Holland received pieces of shell all over his body and face, and was soon rendered unconscious. One side of the carriage was blown out'.

Private Williams, realising the serious nature of the wounds of his companion, pulled the communication cord. The train halted, but with no doctors available, it continued to Fazakerley where the two wounded men were placed in the waiting room awaiting medical assistance. However the ambulance went to the wrong place. Private Holland was still unconscious and Private Williams utilized his first aid training and applied a tourniquet for his own arm and, against advice ran to Fazakerley Hospital for assistance. Private Holland (1434) was conveyed to hospital where he had four inches of his arm amputated, however he succumbed to peritonitis and died on 8 December. He is buried in grave 20, St Thomas Churchyard, Heath Road Extension, Ashton-in-Makerfield. Private Williams was reported as being as well as expected.

A more than satisfactory response arose from Lancashire and Cheshire coal owners and miners who contributed approximately £37,000 for thirty motor ambulances for the BRCS and the St John's Association. As part of a tour of northern towns, on 19 December seven of the ambulances were displayed in the Market Square, Wigan where they were inspected by the Mayor and local dignitaries, followed by lesser mortals from the local mining community; later in the week the fleet went to London to be inspected by King George V.

Back in Wigan, austerity and war weariness made Christmas festivities a rather muted affair in comparison with the previous year.

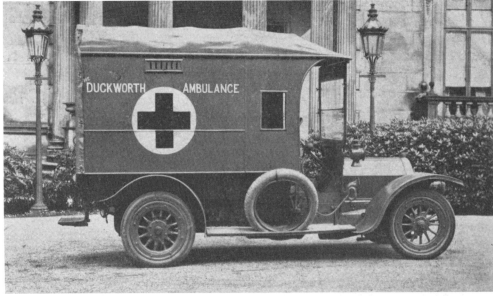

A typical sponsored Great War ambulance.

St Mark's, Wigan Roll of Honour for 1914 – 1915.

At the Infirmary, the North Ward had a large wooden table in the centre covered with a Union flag. Over the fireplace the twenty-four wounded soldiers had made a golden crown surrounded by the flags of the United Kingdom and at dinner they were treated with a sumptuous spread. The Woodland hospital patients had a traditional Christmas dinner followed by entertainment from the Wigan and District Operatic Society.

Over Christmas the surreptitious evacuation of Gallipoli commenced, thus drawing down the curtain on the failed Dardanelles campaign. By 8 January, the 42nd East Lancashire Division along with other units had extricated themselves from Gallipoli. The East Lancashire Division returned to Egypt where it remained until March 1917 when it was transferred to France. The Dardanelles campaign continues to be overshadowed by events on the Western Front despite the presence of some 600,000 British, French and Serbian personnel.

A welcome sight for Wigan's war weary servicemen.

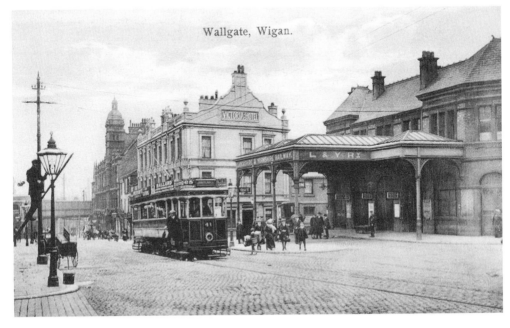

CHAPTER 3

1916
The Realisation

As the New Year dawned those reflecting on the previous year would have gained little consolation from the naval and military manoeuvres. The Western Front was frozen in aspic and the Royal Navy, colloquially referred to as John Bull's teeth, looked increasingly fallible. The realisation dawned that the British Empire was embroiled in a war of attrition in which a British victory could no longer be guaranteed. Against this faltering military backdrop, the home front had evolved into an ever more productive supplier of all manner of essential products ranging from knitted gloves to battleships, but recruitment was in decline. At the beginning of the year, Lord Derby reported that the National Registration details revealed more married men than bachelors had enlisted or attested and that 1,029,231 shirked military service.

The war impacted on families in many ways, inflation was problematic but the prime concern was the fate of loved ones. Rumours might abound followed by heartbreaking news generally received in the form of a telegram.

The death of Lance Corporal Kenealey had not been officially announced but the 19 January *Liverpool Echo* reported:

'The Victoria Cross awarded to Lance Corporal William Keneally, together with a letter signed by George V, was forwarded to Colour Sergeant J.S. Keneally, 361 Bolton Road, Stubshaw, Ashton-in-Makerfield. The letter stated: "It is a matter of sincere regret to me that the death of Private William Keneally deprives me of the pride of personally conferring upon him the Victoria Cross, the greatest of all military decorations."'

As Lord Derby's Military Service Bill began to loom, men attested (signed up) under the Group Scheme and were assured single men would be called up first. After attestation the majority of volunteers returned home to await their call-up papers when the Military Service Act of 27 January 1916 came into force. The first group of Wigan 'Derby soldiers' reported in good numbers and excellent humour and, after completing the Army paperwork, they left for the depot at Ashton-under-Lyne.

The Derby recruits' compliance rankled with the Society of Friends (Quakers) and members of the Socialist Labour Party, who formed the No Conscription Fellowship, and successfully campaigned for a conscience *Lord Derby.* clause in the 1916 Conscription Act. On moral and religious grounds the Conscientious Objectors (COs) refused to break the sixth commandment 'Thou shalt not kill', whatever the circumstances.

The defiant men comprised three categories; the most obstinate were the 'absolutists' who rejected any form of alternative war service that supported war. They refused to take up arms or participate in innocuous and diverse employment encompassing building rifle ranges to sack making, for the end product could be for sandbags or coaling warships. The middle category 'alternativists' also shunned weapons training and soldiering, but were willing to work in occupations not controlled by the army, typically agriculture. The 'non-combatants' did accept military service but in a non-combatant role, several thousand serving in the Royal Army Medical Corps as medics or front-line stretcher-bearers. March 1916 saw the establishment by the army of the Non-Combatant Corps, dubbed the No Courage Corps by the press.

The COs depicted singing love songs to advancing Germans.

The NCC were willing general labourers for any task except handling munitions.

Ultimately, over 16,000 men claimed the right of exemption from military service. More than 6,300 COs were court-martialled and incarcerated. Over 800 spent more than two years in prison enduring privation, hard labour, no talking, a bread and water diet and brutality. The uncompromising regime led to seventy-three deaths, others left prison physically broken or mentally ill. Decades later, a variant of this press gang descendent would force other generations to a stint of military service; British conscription was finally laid to rest in the 1960s.

At the beginning of January the wearing of assorted drilling corps badges was discontinued in favour of the Central Association Proficiency badge.

Under DORA legislation workers' proficiency, namely daily attendance and output, was scrutinised. At the end of January, Wigan resident Richard Southworth, the only fitter employed by the Central Wagon Company, Ince, appeared before magistrates charged

Central Association VTC badge.

with absenting himself from work without notice. The firm was not a Government controlled establishment but produced nothing but war work. Due to the manpower shortage all employees were 'badged' men, so they were aware they worked solely on munitions. Between 5 and 20 January Southworth had lost fifty-six hours and his employer now sought damages. In defence he claimed ill health arising from him having to work a seven-day-week. A fine of £1 was imposed, plus damages. In a similar case Pearson and Knowles, one of the largest colliery firms in the Wigan district reported twenty-two per cent of men were absent from work without notice.

Officials now announced amendments to the licensing laws including a thirty-minute extension of Wigan public house opening hours in alignment with the rest of the county. It was a bitter sweet pill for drinkers as the regulation also prohibited 'no treating', essentially buying someone else a drink of intoxicating liquor. Alcohol on credit became illegal, as did the 'long pull' of extra liquid in a measure of ale and spirits were reduced in strength to between twenty-five and fifty per cent proof. The regulations came into force on 14 February.

The alarming rise in Zeppelin raids prompted the Wigan Emergency Committee in mid-February to distribute posters and newspaper proclamations of the new lighting regulations issued by the Home Office. Screening of lighting proved impractical on the glass-roofed drill hall resulting in the Wigan volunteers suspending evening parades.

During a Wigan Council meeting on 2 March the Mayor advised that 230 volunteers from the building trades had volunteered to form twelve relief parties in the event of a Zeppelin air raid. The St John's Ambulance Brigade would assist casualties and the VAD would be approached. Several councillors complained about the air raid blackout in the town which resulted in indignities to women and was a public danger. Alderman Benson said 'there were accidents and assaults every night'. The town was in darkness but there was a radiating beacon light from the local ironworks [furnaces] although the Wigan Coal and Iron Company made assurances they could damp down in ten minutes. Demands for modifications of the lighting restrictions' were declined as total darkness was a necessity to defeat the Zeppelins. Instances of not turning off lights ninety minutes after sunset abounded, warnings were ignored and the exasperated Chief Constable gave notice that with effect from 7 March any person showing a light in shop windows,

Wigan Coal and Iron Company.

windows of private homes or doorways would be prosecuted. As a result, batches of Wigan residents were summoned under the Restricted Lighting Regulations, in most cases a fine of 12s 6d was imposed.

About this time the Royal Welsh Fusiliers left Ashton Park, where they had been stationed for a few months, and the 5/Manchester left Egypt for France. March also witnessed the first meeting of the Orrell Tribunal under the Military Service Act when fourteen applications for exemption were considered.

Clerical volunteers now applied themselves to implementing the compulsory call-up of various groups or categories of men. The first group called on were single men and childless widowers who had attested under Lord Derby's voluntary scheme. But the administrators' unfamiliarity with the group system resulted in the March call-up of married men instead of attested bachelors. This led to an early March demonstration in the Pavilion by over 4,000 Wigan married men. In May a national outbreak of protests resulted in the introduction of a revised Military Service Act. Regardless of this, the systematic calling up of married men inevitably caused great concern to their dependents in an era when the male was usually the primary wage earner. The introduction of conscription ended the 'chicken hunt' and men from a wide demographic now faced an uncertain future.

The weekly Wigan Military Tribunals between March and June 1916 adjudicated on some 800 cases; after this period the appeals decreased. Up to 14 April, forty-two appeals from decisions of local tribunals in the Wigan area were dealt with by the County Appeal Tribunal at Liverpool under the presidency of the Lord Mayor. Of these, seven were of the Ince Tribunal and all were dismissed, four from the decisions of the Hindley Tribunal were also dismissed. Of the thirty-one appeals against decisions of the Wigan Tribunal, twenty-eight were dismissed and three were allowed two months in which to make arrangements before joining the Army. Those adjudicating at the tribunals were above the military age limit of forty-one.

The same age limitation applied to the newly formed Aspull and Haigh Volunteer Corps who held their first route march one evening in mid-April. They were described as very smart and soldierly with their rifles slung over their shoulders.

This question was frequently asked by tribunals.

The Volunteer Corps were keen to serve their King and country in some capacity, unlike the first batch of Conscientious Objector prisoners charged with failing to report for military service who appeared before a Wigan tribunal on 8 May.

William Welsby, a Corporation labourer stated that his appeal had been dismissed by two tribunals, and Frederick Durkin, a chauffeur, claimed he was entitled to exemption. W. Dakin of Poolstock had reported but refused to sign any paperwork for he never intended to be a soldier, and did not care what the consequences were. And, as he had not signed any papers he did not see why he should be locked up as a criminal. Alfred Stoker, 3 Gidlow Avenue was similarly charged. Harold Smith, 61 Hodges Street, described himself as one of the double-dyed COs and wanted to know why they were not allowed bail at the weekend. The magistrates' clerk said it was in the discretion of the police. Eli Trotter, 37 Darlington Street, trade union secretary, contended the tribunals had not carried out the Act. Richard Worthington, 30 Kenyon Road, said that as a follower of Christ he could not take part in the war. Osmond Bolton, 20 Chancery Street was of the opinion he could not be a deserter since he had not signed any

Women operatives of the Gathurst explosive works. (Courtesy WA&LS)

documents. The bench fined the men 40s to be deducted from their Army pay and they were detained until a military escort arrived.

Life on the Wigan home front was not without its dangers, the canal and coal mines regularly claimed lives and were reported in the press. However censorship prevented journalists from reporting the explosion at the Gathurst Munition Works until January 1919.

The Roburite and Ammonal Explosives Company Limited works at Shevington, over 4 miles north-west of Wigan, manufactured Roburite, a German explosive first trialled in the United Kingdom in 1887. The flameless safety explosive contained no nitro-glycerine, 4ozs would do the work of 1lb of blasting gunpowder and it gave off no noxious fumes allowing miners to re-enter the gallery soon after the charge was fired. Bizarrely wartime adverts in Wigan newspapers offered three products, Roburite No.4, Negro Powder No.2, and Dreadnought. The company also produced TNT in pellet form, this being despatched to other high explosive plants in calico bags transported in covered rail wagons.

The Coroner's inquest heard how on the evening of 15 May 1916 a fire broke out in one of the pans in which the explosive was being made. The operative, William Gore, stopped the motor and used a fire extinguisher until it was expended and went to another shed for an extinguisher. When he returned the entire building, constructed of steel girders with corrugated iron roof and walls and a timber floor covered with asphalt on steel joists, was in flames, and men with hosepipes were attempting to extinguish the fire. The Wigan Fire Brigade arrived promptly and, under the direction of the Chief Constable, attempted to prevent the fire spreading to other explosive material, but a second plant caught fire. Thomas Cooksey, the assistant manager and works engineer, heard four or five small explosions but did not anticipate any further danger. Just after 7pm the smoke changed from a khaki yellow to an intense blue-black, he then told the employees fighting the fire 'Clear out you fellows, for God's sake, clear, jump, run and drop'. As they began running the force of the explosion caught them in the open space between the earthen embankments. The report of the explosion was heard for miles and thousands of spectators, whom the factory sentries kept at a safe distance, were showered in a hail of debris.

The explosion injured twenty-four people and claimed the lives of:

James Edward Barton (34), Quarry House, Appley Bridge, assistant supervisor of bombs.

Charles Edward Eastmead (55), electrician, Margaret Street, Wigan.

Alfred Evans (53) mixer, 3 Charles Street, Orrel, who died the next morning.

William Fleming (27), 5 Gathurst Lane, Shevington.

Frank J.E.O. Lyon (41), trolleyman, 46 Smith Lane, Orrell.

Lance Corporal Jonathan Rhodes (44), Royal Defence Corps, Vicarage Grove, Eccles.

James Shevelton (33), 100 Canal Bank, Crooke.

The cause of the explosion was undetermined but the work of an enemy agent was ruled out. Four days earlier flint stones were discovered in burnt charcoal provided by a Government contractor and undetected stones in the mixing pan were thought to have been the cause of ignition. The destroyed building was not a magazine but finished explosives were temporally stored in the mixing room due to rail congestion. A verdict of accidental death was recorded.

The works manager, Mr Cooksey, was awarded an OBE for saving lives. In autumn 1919, the Chief Constable forwarded to the Home Office the names of Sergeant Rylance and constables Jones and Ainscough for recognition of their conduct at Gathurst, and in 1920 four members of the Wigan Fire Brigade received medals for their conduct at the munitions works.

A few days after the Gathurst explosion, at Platt Bridge near Wigan, the County Coroner held an unrelated inquest into the tragic death of 32-year-old John Robert Kelly of 104 Walthew Lane, Platt Bridge who was discharged from the army as medically unfit.

The enquiry heard that Kelly had brought home as a memento the fuse end off a German shell, which he claimed had killed his commanding officer, and he considered the fuse harmless. On 17 May, Kelly was trying to remove aluminium from the shell to make finger rings, and was using a hammer and chisel to do this. At the fourth blow the shell exploded with terrible force, and splinters of it flew in all directions; Kelly died almost immediately. His wife, whose dress showed about a dozen holes caused by flying shell fragments, was badly injured, and a collier named William Hobbins, a friend of Kelly, received splinters all over his body and was taken to the Wigan

Wartime pit head lasses pose in front of wagons belonging to J. & R. Stone Colleries, Garswood, near Wigan.

Infirmary. A married woman, Sarah Ellen Holding, who was carrying a baby in her arms, and a schoolboy, George Edward Kynaston (13), were also severely wounded. The jury returned a verdict of accidental death.

Bereavement was an experience shared by many Wigan families, industrial accidents were frequent, drowning in the canal and, of course, death in military service were commonplace. Faced with a shortage of male workers employers grudgingly conceded women were capable of more than domestic work.

This was hardly a revelation to generations of Lancashire women who had supplemented family income by working in the collieries. The practice continued until 1842 when the women were prohibited from working underground, instead they worked on the surface grading or sieving coal, or pushing coal-laden skips along rail tracks. They were known as 'pit brow lasses'. At the height of the war, an estimated 2,000 women were employed at South Lancashire coal pits and more were needed to offset the enlisted male surface workers. Their essential contribution to the war effort is generally overshadowed by women employed in a variety of services including street cleaning, postal workers, railway booking clerks, and on public transport.

Arguably the best remembered female workers were those employed in munition factories. In May 1916 a brass brooch in the form of an equilateral triangle engraved 'On War Service' was introduced for female munitions workers. Each received only one badge and 270,000 were issued throughout the war.

Also endeavouring to be of practical use were about ninety men of the Wigan, Hindley and Haigh Volunteers of the Lancashire Volunteer Brigade. In mid-May an inspection by Sir James de Houghton, the Commandant of the County Brigade took place on the rector's field. The Wigan contingent paraded in their smart uniforms while the more recently formed non-uniformed Hindley and Haigh companies wore the red GR armband on their left arm. After dividing into four platoons, the volunteers were put through their paces demonstrating their training in field manoeuvres and a march past. Sir James expressed his satisfaction and advised finding uniforms and arms were under consideration and trusted the men would soon be equipped for home defence.

Munition workers produced any product essential to the war effort.

At home or away the service personnel could find a tranquil haven in one of 8,500 YMCA establishments including Library Street, Wigan. Everywhere, wholesome simple pleasures were provided such as letter writing, teas, and board games. To the rear of the battle zones the YMCA operated from large timber huts. In May a Wigan and district Flag Day raised £600 for a 'Wigan Hut for France'.

As the situation at the front looked increasingly parlous, at the end

Wigan VTC members pose for the camera. (WA&LS)

of May the Mayor of Wigan (Alderman A.S. Hilton JP) issued the following official statement:

> 'That in view of the serious statement made by the Minister of Munitions a few days ago, he is of the opinion the Whitsuntide holidays might be postponed indefinitely, having regard to the urgency of making guns, shells and other munitions in as great a quantity and with as great a speed as possible with the object of bringing the war to an early termination, or at least shorten it.'

A YMCA Hut Fund lapel pin.

The proposal came into fruition as people recognised the urgency for munitions, a message that was forcibly rammed home when the German High Seas Fleet was brought into action on 31 May, to the west of Jutland, off the coast of Denmark.

A postcard of a naval rating taken in a Park Road, Wigan studio.

British vessels had inadequate armour plating and fire control systems, consequently when struck by German shells the magazines on some vessels exploded. Poor gunnery, signalling and a lack of night training compounded the senior service's problems. Thousands of British lives were lost as warships exploded and sank in seconds, including the battle cruiser HMS *Queen Mary*; 1,266 men died including First Class Stoker Thomas Latham whose wife lived at 7 Ashton Road, Golborne. The cruiser HMS *Defence* also exploded and sank and there were no survivors. Amongst the 908 dead were Engine Room Artificer John Henry Lund (38) whose mother resided at 71 Delph Street, Wigan. Also killed was Private Harry Banks (18), a Royal Marine previously employed as a fitter. He and Lund were reported as the only Wigan men who were killed on HMS *Defence*, but other local naval men were reported wounded.

Hospital fundraising continued with vigour following an early June fundraising concert at Woodlands No.2 at which a party of Wigan gentlemen presented a wheelchair to the hospital. A week later, a fundraising event occurred in the Abbey Lakes grounds arranged by

The former Woodlands No.2 auxiliary military hospital.

members of the Abbey Lakes Bowling Club. Wounded soldiers from the Woodlands Group plus the Wigan Infirmary participated in bowls competitions. The event financed a wheelchair for Woodlands No.1, similar to the one recently presented to Woodlands No.2, by gentlemen unable to fight but anxious to do their bit. Weeks later they also provided wheelchairs to Wigan Infirmary.

The sterling efforts of the Wigan and District Division of the British Red Cross Society were declared during their June AGM. New Voluntary Aid Detachments had been formed at Ince (EL/216) and Pemberton and Orrell (EL/220). The strength of the Wigan and District Division amounted to 223 persons, the unit strengths being: EL/50 (Parbold) 20; EL/90 (Wigan) 51; EL/92 (Wigan) 48; EL/96 (Standish) 27; EL/216 (Ince) 45 and EL/220 (Pemberton and Orrell) 32. Over the past year various classes had been held in First Aid, Home Nursing, Invalid Cooking, Hygiene and Sanitation etc. Examinations were held and a gratifying percentage of those sitting had gained certificates issued by the society. Since the 6 October 1914 opening of Woodlands

No.1 to the end of March 1916, 443 men had passed through the division hospitals, each patient spending an average of forty-one days in hospital. The division acknowledged the generosity of Lord Crawford who, in addition to placing Woodlands at their disposal and equipping it as an auxiliary hospital, had donated a total of £949 towards the maintenance of the facility.

Towards the end of the month, the Billinge Workhouse Infirmary became a 300-bed auxiliary military hospital and soon received thirty patients. Miss M. Woodward, the hospital matron, on behalf of her wounded men, appealed to the community for the loan of gramophones, pianos, packs of cards, books, magazines, deck chairs, walking sticks etc. and the public responded magnificently. By 22 July the patient numbers were between 200 and 300 and included wounded from the Somme battles.

Still more men were required to reinforce the front-line soldiers, recruitment officers were now directed to re-assess previously rejected men, leading to claims of Derby Scheme rejects being bullied into the army. It was all a far cry from the vision of Lord Kitchener, who faced criticism over several issues including commissioning too many shrapnel shells instead of high explosives.

The waning star boarded HMS *Hampshire* on a diplomatic mission to Russia and on 5 June the vessel struck a mine off the Orkney coast. Kitchener drowned together with 643 other souls including Stoker First Class William Wood (23), the son of Edward and Margaret Wood of Poolstock, Wigan. The news of Kitchener's demise was received in Wigan with acute sorrow. On 13 June at Wigan Parish Church an impressive service was held in memory of Lord Kitchener and the officers and men who lost their lives following the sinking. The service was attended by the Mayor, Alderman A.S. Hilton JP, local citizens, soldiers, sailors and wounded from the neighbouring hospitals. The Rector, the Reverend Canon R.G. Mathew preached and the Church Lads cadets sounded the Last Post.

But a new spirit of optimism briefly prevailed for all of Britain was alive with talk of the impending 'Big Push' on the Western Front. Neither the timing nor the location were to General Haig's liking but, as the junior partner in the Franco-British alliance, Haig had to bow to French demands for a major British offensive to divert German troops away from the siege of Verdun.

An 'in memoriam' Kitchener postcard.

On 1 July, the opening day of the Somme offensive, 21,392 British Army soldiers were killed or missing presumed dead. Approximately 40,000 more were wounded or maimed and many would die from their wounds months or years later. A large portion of the combatants were the citizen soldiers of Kitchener's Army, including Tom Schofield formerly employed by the Lancashire and Yorkshire Railway Company at Pagefield Goods Station, Wigan. His parents resided at 126 Poolstock Lane, Worsley, Wigan. After being wounded on the opening day of the Battle of the Somme, Private Schofield wrote to his chum from the 1st Southern General Hospital:

Dear Jack, Just a few lines to let you know I was involved in the 'Big Push' and wounded on 1 July, shrapnel wounds in both thighs, my right one being broken. I was then about the German front line. I got into a shell hole, and dressed my wounds, and soon afterwards I noticed our chaps retiring, so I managed to hop along, and got as far as our old front line, which they did not use as it was nearly levelled to the ground. I was laid down when the chap next to me got hit in the shoulder. I had just bandaged him up when I got hit in the right thigh. At night all that could walk went to the dressing station, and I had to stop where I was, and I never saw anyone until the morning of the 7th, which was a bit of luck for the stretcher bearers managed to find me. There were five or six close to where I was as I could hear them shouting. They brought two of us in, and said they would fetch the other chaps later. The worst thing I had to undergo was thirst, I managed to get two bottles of water, but they had gone by the second day. On the third day there was a good shower of rain and I caught the water on a groundsheet then filled the water bottles. With the ground being soft I sank about two feet, and was wet through up to the neck but could not move out of it. But it was fine the day after and I got nearly dry. When I got to the dressing station I got some hot milk and I didn't half give it sock. I have been looked after fine in France and here. I arrived in England 14 July. My wounds are doing fine and I am in the pink. Hoping to find you well.

Your old friend Tommy

We now fast forward to September 1967 when a muddy wasteland behind Ince Moss Colliery became the setting for a re-enactment of the 1 July 1916, filmed by Granada Television for their serialisation of *Inheritance* which was based on the novels by Phyllis Bentley. Some fifty extras in full battle dress, camera crews and technical staff and child actors participated in three days filming. Over £1,000 was expended adding realism to the location. The Moss sprouted broken trees, barbed wire and water-filled holes festooned with dead bodies; specially laid charges exploded with a crash loud enough to wake the dead in the nearby old cemetery. An interested bystander 77-year-old Peter Unsworth, who served with 5/Manchester on the Western Front, commented: 'It compares well with the real thing; the landscape is typical of what I saw in France when it rained. But the firing was a lot noisier there. You couldn't hear yourself think, never mind talk, when the big guns were going.'

The Somme battle was a week old when the Ministry of Munitions attempted to quash rumours of the dangers to men and women employed handling TNT explosive in shell filling factories. His Majesty's Medical Inspector agreed high explosives may cause skin irritation but this stopped after the work was discontinued. Of the many thousands of reported illnesses he falsely claimed only a few isolated cases were serious or fatal. The idle talk was affecting the labour supply at new factories; any person spreading the rumour could, under DORA, receive a penalty of six months jail with hard labour and a fine of £100. His opinion conveniently ignored the fact that prolonged exposure to the sulphuric acid in Trinitrotoluene (TNT) can seriously damage the immune system and vital organs and lead to discolouring of the skin. Such women were nicknamed canaries.

Also taking up a new role was Earl Crawford (formerly Lord Balcarres and now known in the House of Lords as Baron Wigan) who had enlisted in April 1915 as a private soldier in the Royal Army Medical Corps and served incognito in France as an orderly at a Casualty Clearing Station for 14 months. In July 1916 he was serving in France as a second lieutenant (having finally agreed to a commission) when he accepted the position of President of the Board of Agriculture and Fisheries. On 12 August he made his first public appearance at the annual cattle and foal show of the Haigh, Aspull and Blackrod Ploughing Society and Foal Show held on his lordship's Haigh estate. In a portent of things to come he said, 'the war is placing a severe strain on the agricultural resources of the country, more especially regarding livestock, and it was essential farmers should improve the character and worth of their herds'. To offset the shortage of farm hands, during the summer local scouts of various troops helped in farm work.

The German submarine campaign was exerting a tighter stranglehold on British imports, consequently demand frequently exceeded supply and food prices continued to spiral upwards. Some resorted to petty theft to circumvent shortages and targeted particular fields now watched by plain clothes policeman. They caught a married man who had five children stealing 6lb of potatoes from a Wigan Coal and Iron Company field, where another man stole 10d worth of potatoes. Each offender received a 20s (£1) fine and 2s 6d witness costs as a deterrent to others.

Law enforcement also suffered manpower deficiencies; by January

By George - a beastly bomb - what!

Special Constables were the butt of countless jokes.

1917 Wigan Borough Police had forty-four officers serving in the military; four had been killed. In November 1915, Wigan raised special constables from starred men or those over military age, however the specials complained on a busy evening in King Street people would take no notice of them. Possibly to give the specials an air of authority, in May 1917 the Watch Committee approved supplying the borough's 145 Special Constables with soft felt caps with a badge in front.

To assuage 'khaki fever' and prevent discharged men in civilian clothes being scorned as cowards, on 12 September the King approved the issue of the Silver War Badge. This was issued to officers and men of the British, Indian and Overseas Forces who had served at home or abroad since 4 August 1914, and who, on account of age or physical infirmity arising from wounds or sickness caused by military service, had, in the case of officers retired or relinquished their commissions, or in the case of men, been discharged from the services.

Silver War Badge.

In the absence of the welfare state, able-bodied discharged combatants returned to civilian occupations including the expanding motorised vehicle sector. Assembly production lines were as yet futuristic, although some commercial vehicle chassis manufacturers made their own bodies, the majority had arrangements with a principal coachbuilder. In mid-September the Wigan Motor Bodies Company re-located to large two-storey premises where each finished body was lowered by means of a first floor hoist onto the chassis situated on the ground floor. The company produced twenty finished coach (lorry) bodies per week and were engaged in a large order of motor vehicles for the Government.

Munitions contractors and military installations were prime targets for marauding airships. Lancashire was spared until the night of 25 September when the German airship *L21* ineffectually dropped scores of bombs on Rawtenstall and Holcombe, then headed for Bolton believing the town to be Derby. The airship, guided by the glow from Bolton foundries, dropped twenty-three bombs primarily on a working class terraced street. Thirteen people, including two babies died, a further nine were seriously injured. The 179m long airship returned unchallenged to its Hamburg base.

In the wake of the raid the Wigan Chief Constable, fearing a similar aerial bombardment, issued ARP posters and placed large notices in the local papers reiterating the ARP Regulations and advised that these were the only protective measures the borough had against air raids. The public negligence in observing the regulations was causing the police a great deal of unnecessary trouble and those failing to observe the subdued lights regulations would be fined 10s.

Fiscal demands were behind a five-week long strike by 2,000 card room and blowing room operatives employed in Wigan mills. This led to an additional 1,000 workers dependent on the strikers' production being laid off, forcing many to seek employment in other towns. The dispute ended at the start of October when employers agreed to pay a five per cent increase in wages.

Voluntarism was still much in evidence. On 3 November at the Ince Public Hall, St John Ambulance Association certificates were presented to thirty-six ladies of the Moss Hall Division Ambulance Association; of these fourteen volunteered to go overseas. Since the inception of the association twenty-five male members had joined the forces and raised £100 for an Abram bed at the base hospital in France. The division intended to contribute £100 a year to fund its upkeep.

Other unsung volunteers were the Wigan gentlemen who rendered civil service by the loan of their motor cars for transporting wounded personnel to hospital or on day outings – fresh air then being the panacea for most ailments. A November meeting in connection with the National Motor Volunteer Movement took place in the Old Council Chamber where a speaker

A St John Ambulance volunteer.

explained that while previously all efforts had been voluntary, the King was soon expected to give assent to official recognition, requiring members to enrol and take the oath in a similar manner to the VTC. The formation of a Wigan and District Motor Corps was decided upon unanimously.

As the third wartime Christmas approached, George V issued the following message to his soldiers, sailors and the sick and wounded:

'I send you, my sailors and soldiers, hearty wishes for Christmas and New Year. My grateful thoughts are ever with you for victories gained, for hardships endured, and for your unfailing cheeriness. Another Christmas has come round and we are still at war. But the Empire, confident in you, remains determined to win.

May God bless and protect you. George R.I.'

TO THE WOUNDED
'At this Christmastide the Queen and I are thinking more than ever of the sick and wounded among my soldiers and sailors. From our hearts we wish them strength to bear their sufferings, speedy restoration to health, a peaceful Christmas and many happy years to come.

George R.I.'

His Majesty King George V.

CHAPTER 4

1917
Seeing it Through

The subjects of Kaiser Wilhelm II of Germany were equally bowed and bloodied and committed to a war of attrition. The Kaiser and George V were grandsons of Queen Victoria, but the warring cousins now had something else in common, their subjects faced food shortages. Britain's two-and-a-half year distant naval blockade of German ports had a severe impact on food imports and war materials, however both cargos clandestinely passed through neutral ports. On the other hand the Royal Navy was at its wits end on how to deal with submarines preying on the merchantmen. Britain's maritime trade links were becoming increasingly endangered.

In December, German attempts to negotiate a peace settlement were dismissed by the Allies, this rejection combined with the blockade, brought about a catastrophic shift in sea policy. The German government proclaimed from midnight 31 January that no Allied vessels would be permitted access to a Barred Zone extending from a line drawn from Flamborough Head to Terschelling, an island off the Netherlands, and between Ushant off the French coast near Brest and Land's End. Territorial waters of neutral countries were observed, but any vessel entering the prohibited waters of the North Sea or the Atlantic near the British Isles faced destruction.

Effective from 1 January, sugar was rationed to half a pound per head, while available. At the same time millers were ordered to use standard flour instead of white, and extract from the wheat some seventy-four per cent of grain; at the end of the month a further five per cent was demanded through extra milling or the addition of oats or barley. Following the introduction of the 'national loaf', white bread was a thing of the past, and the use of sugar or chocolate for the outside dressing of cakes was prohibited.

As food shortages proliferated the nation began to 'Dig for Victory', by utilising sections of municipal parks and waste ground. In January, the DORA-empowered council took over waste land with a view to assisting the food supply and arranged for its cultivation by any persons

Digging for victory.

or society. The parks superintendent advised two acres were available at Alexander Park, and a half-acre by the brook at Mesnes Park if it was drained. Schools were encouraged to instruct pupils in the growing of potatoes and foodstuffs and letters were sent to land owners in the borough requesting their sites be placed at the Allotment Committees disposal. At Beech Hill, some forty acres of land and fifteen acres at Platt Lane belonging to the Thicknesse Trust were freely loaned for growing potatoes. Land near the service reservoir at Boars Head and also Warrington Road was also made available. A representative of The Wigan Coal and Iron Company offered land near the golf course, Hall Lane and off Ladies Lane, also ground near the bridges at a nominal rent; they were prepared to plough and separate each allotment by a ring fence.

Barriers preventing the enlistment of 'starred' workers were rescinded near the close of January. The Government decided that in view of the urgent needs of the Army and of the reduction in the export of coal and economies in use at home, a certain number of men could be released from the mines for military service. The temporary exemptions granted to the men who entered the mining industry after 14 August 1915, having been engaged in other occupations, and to unskilled men working on the surface, were cancelled. The exemption of men who had persistently worked short time without reasonable cause was reviewed by the Colliery Recruiting Courts; travelling medical boards also visited the collieries. As an example of their intervention, weeks later the County Tribunal held at Liverpool Town Hall reviewed the exemptions that had previously been granted. Included were nineteen coal and spinning industries men from the Wigan district. A number of exemptions were cancelled and the men ordered to join the Army immediately, a few others were granted a short extension presumably to put their affairs in order.

The war of attrition intensified on 1 February when the German Government announced that it would 'henceforth tolerate no hospital ship' in defined areas and would, contrary to the Geneva Convention, treat hospital ships as legitimate targets. The neutral Americans were becoming increasingly fractious. Following the German decision to conduct unrestricted submarine warfare, America severed diplomatic links with Germany, thus taking a minute step towards war with Germany. From mid-March American merchant ships followed the

Anglo-French lead and commenced fitting their merchant ships with stern-mounted defensive guns.

Vessels on the internal waterways were far removed from the submarine menace, but they played an important role in the transportation of materials. The Government, in an effort to relieve the pressure on railways, had previously taken over 1,360 miles of railway owned and controlled waterways. About 4,670 miles of canals and navigations then existed in the United Kingdom. At the end of February a regulation under DORA enabled the Board of Trade to take possession of any non-railway owned canal in the country. A month later at the half-yearly meeting of the Leeds and Liverpool Canal Company it was announced tolls and freight revenue on the 145 mile long canal had diminished by £4,000 compared to the same period of the previous year, when figures were also low. The losses were mainly due to a reduced carriage of goods in the company boats arising from the shortage of boatmen and having to withdraw boats from service. Out of 154 steamers, tugs and boats, sixty-eight were laid up due to a shortage of crews.

But there seemed no lack of financial investments; discussions in the House of Commons revealed new money subscribed to the War Loan had exceeded £700,000,000. Small investors purchasing War Savings Certificates were offered good rates of interest and proved popular in Wigan. Between New Year's Day and 17 February the Wigan head post office and district offices handled £35,753 in War Saving Certificates.

Acquiring certification of death for a munition worker was a more protracted affair, possibly due to the earlier mentioned DORA dictat. The Wigan Borough Coroner's inquest began in mid-February and continued until April on Margaret Ann Silcock (22), a single woman who died at her home 1 Wrights Yard, off Wigan Lane, Wigan under peculiar circumstances. She was previously employed in a spinning mill, but spent the last eight months working in an undisclosed shell-filling factory outside Wigan, and for seven weeks had felt unwell. After spending three weeks in the cottage hospital, she returned to work and was given work sewing. After three weeks, she left work, and after remaining briefly at her lodgings, she returned home on 8 February, with a companion, Dr Macallan, who attended her until she died. At the inquest Dr Macallan was of the opinion pneumonia was the direct

ONE OF THE LITTLE 'DUCKS'
WHO'S HELPING TO HATCH THE SHELLS

Munition worker sitting on shell.

cause of death, the primary cause being TNT poisoning. Dr Christine Barrowman, the lady doctor at the shell factory, disagreed with the diagnosis and attributed the death to phthisis (tuberculosis). The coroner adjourned the enquiry pending a post mortem. Samples of organs forwarded to the Ministry of Munitions showed lung lesions attributed to war work. Dr Barrowman, who was unable to attend the enquiry verdict, bowed to the opinion of the medical experts. Silcock had died in the service of her country and unwittingly made as great a sacrifice as those killed in the front-line.

On the Western Front, commencing the last week in February, German forces began a tactical withdrawal to the Hindenburg Line, a system of supporting fortresses in parts some 20 miles (32 km) to the rear of their original front. As they covertly withdrew they operated a scorched earth policy, poisoned water supplies, left booby-traps and destroyed the infrastructure.

At the same time in Mesopotamia (Iraq) the British launched an offensive in the direction of Baghdad. Also in March George V, still fearful of invasion, appealed to his subjects not on military service to either join the volunteers or be categorised as vulnerable as women and children.

In the House of Commons, the First Lord of the Admiralty reported in the first eighteen days of the month that 134 British, Allied and neutral ships had been lost and described the submarine menace as grave and the problem still unresolved. On land, gains were made on the Somme and the British captured Baghdad. Another British force, in what became known as the First Battle of Gaza, unsuccessfully attacked the Turkish province of Palestine. It would take until December before the British entered Jerusalem.

Another U-boat victim.

In Lancashire the National Motor Volunteer Corps now became the Lancashire Motor Volunteers and had received the assent of the King. All Wigan motorists were invited to a meeting on 5 March to enrol in the new arm of national service. Several weeks later regular parade notices appeared in the press declaring every driver and orderly was expected to attend company drill conducted each Wednesday evening at the drill hall. No.3 Section under Sergeant P.J. Conroy was detailed to air raid and hospital duties; even so, the nation clamoured for more community volunteers.

The fledgling National Service programme led to yet another local committee being established in the borough in response to the stirring utterances of Prime Minister David Lloyd George:

'Enrol today for National Service and help to defeat the grimmest menace that every threatened this country.

Every time you buy food in a shop or eat it at table say to yourself that our merchant sailors have died and are dying to bring it to you. It is bought not merely with money but blood.

If you can use a spade, if you are good at gardening – go on the land at once. Go to help our dangerously low stocks. Go now while there is still time for the spring sowings to yield your summer and winter food. In a few weeks time it will be too late. . .'

Given the urgency of the situation the new committee leapt into action. Boy Scouts, Church Lads and other organizations delivered to each home a National Service Campaign leaflet entitled 'Twelve reasons why every able-bodied man should enlist for National Service' accompanied by a letter from Wigan's Mayor urging every man from eighteen to sixty-one-years to enrol on the enclosed form and offer himself in whatever role the nation could utilise his service or skill to the benefit of the state. The clergy of all denominations were requested to make a pulpit appeal on Sunday, 25 March for National Service volunteers. Public meetings followed in Queens Hall and at Hindley.

In Russia deep-rooted social tensions, exacerbated by shortages of food and fuel, paved the way for revolution and on 15 March Tsar Nicholas II abdicated. Amid increasing concerns over Russia's willingness to prosecute war on the Eastern Front, on 9 April the British attacked German positions in Artois, east of Arras and the Canadian

HMHS Asturius

Corps captured Vimy Ridge, but at Bullecourt it would take days to pierce the Hindenburg Line and the advance gradually became deadlocked and dragged on to early May.

At sea, the Germans carried out their threat to sink a hospital ship. HMHS *Asturias*, formerly of the Royal Mail Steam Packet Company, was the largest cross-Channel hospital, having cots for 895 patients. Shortly before midnight on 20 March, as she steamed off the Devonshire coast, mercifully with no wounded onboard, *Asturias* was attacked by a torpedo from a German submarine. The explosion blew the stern off the ship, destroyed the engine room and plunged the ship into darkness. Despite the damage *Asturius* managed to beach herself. Germany justified her first deliberate attack of a hospital ship by alleging the British used the vessels for carrying munitions in breach of the Geneva Convention. The international symbol of the Red Cross no longer guaranteed neutrality.

During eight weeks of unrestricted naval warfare, over 500 merchant vessels were lost at the start of the great shipping annihilation, and the arrival and departure of neutral cargo vessels plummeted to a quarter of the equivalent months in the previous year. The Western Approaches became a graveyard for ships, German predictions of starving Britain into surrender within five months looked increasingly likely. Evidently the Royal Navy anti-submarine tactics, comprising offensive patrols and barrages across the English Channel and the Mediterranean Otranto Straits, were ineffective. Sighting a U-boat, never mind sinking one, proved exceptionally difficult, for submarine detection technology was still in its infancy.

However the campaign by Brigadier Owen Wolley that resulted in three additional 'Lancashire Landing' Victoria Crosses being awarded to his fellow Lancashire Fusiliers was a success. The 13 March 1917 *London Gazette* announcement reiterated the original 24 August citation. The awards to Major Cuthbert Bromley (since drowned), Sergeant Edward Stubbs (died of wounds) were posthumous. The third recipient, Lance Corporal Grimshaw had his Distinguished Conduct Medal (DCM) cancelled and replaced with Britain's premier gallantry award.

Corporal, later Sergeant John Elisha Grimshaw VC was the only true Lancastrian among the 'six before breakfast' VCs. He was born in Abram, Wigan and worked for many years as a carpenter at Cross, Tetley and Co's pits in the Wigan coalfields. He enlisted in 1912, and was a Lancashire Fusiliers private serving in India when war broke out. After his award of the DCM, Abram township presented him with a gold watch and chain, the inscription on the watch being 'Presented to

CORP. (NOW SERGT.)
GRIMSHAW,
Lancashire Fusiliers.

SERGT. F. E. STUBBS,
Lancashire Fusiliers.

CAPT. (TEMP. MAJOR)
BROMLEY, C.B.,
Lancashire Fusiliers.

Three Victoria Cross heroes.

Sgt J.E. Grimshaw for conspicuous bravery at Cape Helles on 25 April 1915, March 10th 1916'.

A far more prestigious investiture occurred in mid March 1917 when Grimshaw attended Buckingham Palace to receive the Victoria Cross from King George V. On 2 April the local hero made a guest appearance at the Wigan Hippodrome recruitment event aimed at young miners. During the proceedings Grimshaw VC received a £5 note from the Mayor and a similar gift from the double act of Max Everard and Miss Zona Vevey.

Since the outbreak of war 150,000 men had gone into the pits, 573,000 men of military age were thus exempt from military service; of these no fewer than 160,000 were unmarried men under thirty-one years of age. At the expense of coal production a concerted effort began to comb out miners. By arrangement with the Miners Federation, until 8 May the coal industry was granted a voluntary system of recruitment that

The Victoria Cross

allowed miners of military age to select the regiment of their choice. When the deadline passed recruiting officers called up men who had been released by the colliery tribunals and each day local men were sent to Seaforth to be medically examined. Those failing the medical were allowed to return to the colliery.

Inevitably local miners figured strongly in the 8,000 to 10,000 local men serving with the colours, of these over eighty former employees of two collieries in Pemberton – Orrell and Norley – had made the supreme sacrifice. The council now began discussing a Roll of Honour in the form of a memorial cross erected in a prominent part of the town, or the less popular proposal of erecting a memorial workshop for the benefit of maimed soldiers and sailors.

Convalescing servicemen were not forgotten, for in early April work on the Ashton-in-Makerfield Convalescent Hospital neared completion. The hospital was 'situated in a beautifully wooden part of Garswood Park, which was placed at their service by Lady Gerard. . . quite a little town of huts had grown up'. The first patients were expected during Easter week, Colonel Broome-Giles CB and staff were intent on getting the men in their charge as fit as possible with the least lapse of time. Their therapy involved physical training of every variety and, to prevent boredom, a competitive element was introduced. Regular sporting tournaments were held, the most popular being the boxing bouts; the tournaments were open to visitors who made a donation towards the hospital overheads.

In the ongoing drive to stave off starvation, corporations were empowered under the provisions of the Cultivation of Lands Order, 1917 (No.2) to take compulsory possession of land suitable for agriculture or grazing. All manner of sites were being turned over to cultivation; typically a cricket field used by St Mark's Church became an allotment, at Ince, grass land at the Westwood Sewage Works and behind the Pumping Station at Fir Tree was offered for a peppercorn rent. By early April, Wigan had 436 allotments under cultivation, twenty-three by schoolchildren. Houses on the Blundells Estate had about 230 gardens, of these 150-180 were turned over to agriculture. On 7 June, at Standish Lower Ground, forty allotments each 300 yards square were opened, they were all situated within a few minutes' walk of Martland Mill Bridge along the brook marking the boundary between Standish and Wigan. The allotment holders were mainly miners residing in houses overlooking the ground. Throughout the district people cut down hedges to make room for vegetables in valiant attempts to bolster Britain's diminishing food stocks as only six weeks of corn supply remained in the country.

At this juncture the German submarines had almost severed Britain's maritime trade routes. But, spurred on by rogue attacks against American vessels, on 6 April 1917, President Wilson received approval to declare war on Germany, followed by a declaration on 7 December against Austria-Hungary.

Joseph Gregson of Lafferty, Ohio, USA wrote to the *Wigan Observer*:

'We are O.K., but we can come to your aid. I am forty-five-years-of-age, but I can keep three Germans back, and there are a hundred more to come with me. I have several nephews in the front line in France. I am a Wigan man, I have grey hair but I have brains too. We are 1,000 strong, young and old and willing to fight for our flag. We are all Lower Incers and Spring Viewers and call on us you will find us O.K. Your paper has been on our table for twenty to thirty years.'

But it would take months before the first drafts of 'doughboys' arrived in France. Meanwhile, in mid April, the French General Robert Nivelle launched a major offensive between Soissons and Reims, a distance of approximately 40 miles (64 km). The majority of the troops were tasked with capturing the series of densely-wooded ridges, forming the Chemin des Dames. German artillery fire and entrenched machine guns decimated the French and the offensive resulted in deadlock. Having sustained some 187,000 casualties, with their self-esteem shattered, some French front line units mutinied. With the French army in meltdown, the offensive was aborted on 9 May. Until French morale recovered the British had no recourse but to engage the enemy at every opportunity.

The Admiralty had opposed the traditional wartime safeguard of escorting merchant men, but in February, pressure from Admirals Jellicoe and Duff brought about the first 'modern age' controlled sailings (or convoy) by escorting colliers to France. By the end of May, only nine of the 4,000 coastal ships using the system had been sunk. And, on the evening of 10 May, the initial homeward-bound convoys departed from Gibraltar and the United States of America. Their successful United Kingdom arrival led to the implementation in August of the convoy system. Mercantile shipping losses of twenty-five per cent in February steadily reduced as more escort vessels became available and by the end of the year the losses were a sustainable one percent.

Nonetheless the food situation was critical, at the beginning of May, George V signed a proclamation exhorting people to lessen their consumption of wheat and to practise the greatest frugality in the use of all types of grain. Families were encouraged to reduce their consumption of bread by one quarter and those who kept horses were forbidden to feed oats or other grain unless they had a specific licence from the food controller. The king also requested all churches to read the proclamation each Sunday for four successive weeks.

In their quest for more soldiers, the Government summoned all previous military rejects for re-examination, but bone-fide agriculturists were excused. The shortage of men led to an increase in the military upper age restriction. Locally the Army Service Corps advertised for horsemen between forty-one to sixty years of age to voluntarily enlist to be posted to Remount Departments. Experienced coachmen, grooms, carters, jockeys and hunt servants were to attend the Wigan Recruiting Office.

EAT LESS BREAD.

THREE SLICES AMONG FOUR OF US
THANK GOODNESS THERE'S NO MORE OF US.

Eat less bread

The depletion of the male population impacted on the community in many ways. In the absence of Driver J. Bolton who was on active service, his two younger sisters, Ethel Bolton (15) and Jessie Bolton (13) carried on his barber and shaving business at 7 Orrell Road, Lamberhead Green. Ethel was probably the youngest barber in the country, her sister being the shaving lather girl.

Also doing his bit was the Wigan Borough Engineer and Surveyor who received a letter from France acknowledging the help Wigan had given in repairing French roads. The surveyor had a hundred vacancies for General Labourers, Steam Roller Drivers, Carpenters etc. for overseas work for men of military age. Good rates of pay and separation allowance were offered by the Surveyor's Office – nearly 200 men responded.

Corporal Melling one of the employees of Wigan Corporation wrote:

'I find road making in France very different to home style. Our work consists chiefly of repairing roads that are not fit to carry heavy traffic of a heavy nature and make them fit to bear the

The former Sailors' and Soldiers' Rest Rooms are now a hairdressers.

enormous heavy traffic necessary to maintain our army in the field. We have to make use of any material we can get.'

His thoughts were echoed by Wigan's Mayor who appealed for donations of small furniture, curtains, crockery etc. for a new war charity. Servicemen arrived in the town after long hours of travel and, owing to restricted railway arrangements, had a long wait before proceeding on their journey. At night they waited around cold and miserable as there was nowhere to get refreshments. Loaned premises at 53 Wallgate, adjacent to two railway stations, were officially opened as the Sailors' and Soldiers' Rest Rooms in mid-May by Lady Gerard. The benevolent lady regularly featured in the press, unlike a lowly munitions worker who received a few column inches and a century later the following tribute.

Bertha MacIntosh (22), a munition worker of 30 Stonecross Lane, Lowton died in the Wigan Infirmary on 19 May. At the inquest into her death the deceased's father informed the Wigan Borough Coroner his daughter previously had the best of health and worked at the toffee works in Lowton, but left home in January for work in a northern munitions factory. He had not seen her until she returned home on 20 April; her eyes were yellow, and she was sleepy and unable to retain food and rambled away in bed. Her condition deteriorated, after seeking medical advice she was admitted to the Wigan Infirmary but died the next day. The post-mortem was attended by seven doctors who agreed the cause of death was acute atrophy of the liver due to TNT poisoning.

In the killing fields spades were almost as important as rifles, especially in West Flanders where British engineers were busy driving twenty tunnels (the Germans discovered one) towards Messines Ridge, south of Ypres. This natural stronghold, held by the Germans since 1914, dominated the British lines, until 0310 hours on 7 June, when nineteen mine heads crammed with 600 tons of explosives blasted the Germans off the ridge. The next day German counter-attacks were repulsed, subsequent counter-attacks decreased in intensity and by 14 June the British held the entire ridge and delivered a desperately needed boost to national morale, removing a key obstacle to an impending British advance.

A month later a letter from Jas Dolan referring to this mining operation appeared in the *Wigan Observer*:

'I and three other local boys have had a good go of it for rather a long spell, as we left the infantry in November 1915, and joined the engineers [tunnelling], and have been at it ever since. I know you will be glad to hear that a few of the Wigan boys were there to represent the well known colliery town. Well I must say a few words about myself. Before joining the army in September 1914, I was working at Princess Pit, Pemberton Collieries, and resided at 40 Goose Green, Wigan, so I have got to my own occupation all right.'

Others readily accepted a change of occupation or took the opportunity to escape from household drudgery. The Women's Army Auxiliary Corps (WAAC) was formed in early 1917, for duties other than nursing. Some 6,000 members of the Women's Legion worked in army kitchens,

WAAC recruiting advertisement.

camps and canteens or filled male roles as motor drivers, store-women, telephone operators and a myriad of other functions and it became obvious that a co-ordinating organisation was required. The WAAC arose from a combination of the Women's Legion and all other societies concerned with women's army work. In Wigan the National Service Department advertised for women to be employed in the pay department as clerks, typists and canteen workers, selection boards were held in Liverpool on 11, 12 and 13 June. By the following year, nationally nearly 40,000 women had enrolled including some 7,000 who served in the rear areas of the Western Front filling roles that released men for front line duty, albeit on a reduced pay to their male counterparts. The women's section of the National Service scheme also comprised the Women's Land Army, the VAD and the Timber Section.

Women also worked as conductors on trams increasingly monopolised by incapacitated servicemen who filled the trams to capacity thereby preventing other passengers and munition workers from boarding. The Tramways Committee heard on the Orrell route soldiers going to Wigan would board the car for Abbey Lakes at Orrell Post and fill the car on the outward and return journey. The same applied on the Ashton route resulting in batches of miners having to be left at Park Lane. A conductor stated that of the fifty wounded soldiers on his tram, only four agreed to pay the fare and he was too ashamed to ask for payment. Mindful of their responsibilities to ratepayers the committee resolved to allow on any one journey six wounded soldiers but they would travel free.

Also freely giving service were the 160 members of the Wigan and District Workroom operating from commodious loaned premises at Hope Schools. On 5 July the workroom celebrated its second anniversary having opened for over 200 days from 10.30 to 5.00pm every Wednesday and Thursday. The output was considered as one of the largest for any district in Lancashire producing over 83,000 articles;

Women making bandages for hospitals.

typically surgical dressings, bandages, swabs etc. were made and despatched to base hospitals and auxiliary hospitals.

Patients from the Woodlands hospitals were invited to a sell-out mid-July matinee at the Wigan Hippodrome arranged as a fund raiser for the Wigan Motor Volunteers squadron. The star attraction was George Formby (1875-1921) who was known as the Wigan Nightingale as during his act he used a bronchial cough to comedic effect. Formby made three appearances in character and auctioned several items for corps funds. Patients were afterwards entertained to tea, followed by a concert at the Queens Hall by the ladies of the Wigan Wesleyan Mission.

Several days later the squadron, joined by private motor cars from the district, took the patients from Wigan Infirmary and the Woodlands group on another Sunday afternoon trip to Rivington. The cars assembled at Market Square then departed to hospitals to collect the wounded continuing the journey to Worthington, where they were joined by the cars from The Beeches, Standish. All thirty-four cars proceeded to Rivington where tea was provided followed by a tour of the gardens and grounds of Lord Leverhulme.

As these genteel outings took place, on the Western Front a fortnight-long British preliminary bombardment involving 2,000 field guns and 1,000 howitzers pulverised German defences across 18 kilometres of front in readiness for the Third Battle of Ypres. As an indication of Britain's ability to bite back, the barrage expended some 4.24 million shells.

On 31 July, the officers' whistles blew, and the men went 'over the top' to meet their destiny. Despite Haig's meticulous preparations to capture Belgium ports occupied by Germans, early successes foundered against in-depth German defences, and then the German ally – the rain – intervened. The bombardments had destroyed the watercourses, flooded shell holes became death traps, streams burst their banks, and the ground became a quagmire, paralysing the advance of British, Canadian and Australian troops. But they stoically pressed on in the mistaken belief the Germans were on the verge of collapse. The notorious offensive continued for several months, culminating in the Battle of Passchendaele. The fight for the village continued until 6 November when Canadian troops entered the demolished village, the British offensive then ceased.

On the home front, Wigan Corporation acquired a historic mansion known as White Hall, then located at the Rodney Street end of Millgate. In late August the property opened as a workshop for 100 blind local residents. They were taught mat making, boot and shoe mending, stocking knitting, plain sewing and other wage-earning handicrafts. Special consideration was given to soldiers and sailors blinded in the war and an exhibition of proficiency in Braille shorthand and type-writing was given by Private Cuthbert Molloy, of Wigan, a miner and former prominent forward in the Wigan Northern Union team. Molloy was rendered sightless in battle and was trained at St Dunstan's workshops for the blind. A few days after White Hall opened on 18 August the latest local flag day endeavoured to raise £1,000 to relieve the workshop committee of financial responsibility.

Another newly appointed body, namely the Wigan Food Control Committee, came into being at the beginning of September. The fifteen members included the Mayor, two councillors and assorted tradesmen and retailers, and in class conscience, war ravaged Britain, Walter Mason represented the working class.

And, following a meeting of the council War Emergency and Street Lighting Committee they agreed to the Chief Constable's foolhardy request for more street lighting contrary to air raid precautions. A two-week experiment commenced 17 September when the wartime introduced British Standard Time (BST) ended. The trial involved the restoration of all electric lights in the street, King Street Arcade was to be lit electrically, all churches had to extinguish lights by 8pm and shops were allowed full lighting inside but shaded lights in the window. Gas lights no longer required painting, and all gas lamps on street corners were illuminated to reduce accidents. A month later fifty-eight streets were lit by 160 lights, the presupposition for electric as opposed to gas lighting being that electric lighting could be promptly switched off at the power station on receipt of an air raid warning – if they received one!

In mid-September Wigan householders who had completed the mandatory sugar application forms began to receive their sugar rationing cards distributed by the Food Control Office, 11 Standish Gate. Helping to counteract food shortage was the responsibility of all as demonstrated by twenty-four boys, the headmaster and assistant from Up-Holland Grammar School. The group went to Keelby, 8 miles

YOUR SUGAR OR YOUR LIFE !!

Sugar became a much sought after product.

from Grimsby where they worked on local farms for fifteen days pulling and stacking beans – destined for bread in 1918 – turnip weeding, heaping and stacking, oats, wheat and barley and received £35 in wages.

The food situation remained critical, but the Royal Navy had a rare stroke of luck in September when the German mine-laying submarine *UC44* struck a mine, and sank off the Waterford coast. On salvaging the vessel, the Admiralty recovered vital intelligence including how U-boats, under cover of darkness, passed over the English Channel anti-submarine nets. The nets were transgressed by 253 submarines in ten months, this reduced journey time to the Western Approaches by eight days in comparison to the North Sea route, saved fuel, and extended by eight days the submarines' patrol. However, admiralty staff failed to deploy counter measures. Finally, on 15 December the First Sea Lord lost his patience and ordered the bolt-hole to be closed. Surface patrols were increased and the barrage was brightly illuminated at night by searchlights; the new measures immediately had a significant impact on German submarine operations.

The war at sea may have shifted in favour of the Allies, but on land the troops were fighting to a standstill. Amongst the millions of combatants was Thomas Woodcock who was born at Belvoir Street, Wigan and educated at St Patrick's Roman Catholic Church. He worked for many years as a miner at the Hindley Green pits of John Scowercroft and Co. Although in a 'starred occupation', Woodcock and friends joined the Irish Guards in May 1915, and after five months training went to France.

On 17 October 1917 the *London Gazette* announced the award of the Victoria Cross to Lance Sergeant Moyney and Private Woodcock of 2/Irish Guards. Moyney's citation differed slightly to Woodcock's:

'On 12/13 September 1917, north of Broenbeek, Belgium when an advanced post had been held for ninety-six hours and was finally forced to retire, the lance sergeant [Moyney] in charge of the party and Private Woodcock covered the retirement. After crossing the stream themselves Private Woodcock heard cries for help behind him – he returned and waded into the stream amid a shower of bombs and rescued another member of the party whom he carried across open ground in daylight towards our front line, regardless of machine-gun fire.

Sergeant Moyney and Private Woodcock VC.

Both employers and communities took pride in their local heroes as exemplified in the forty-fourth AGM of the Pearson and Knowles Coal and Iron Company held on 4 October. The number of employees joining the colours amounted to 4,162, the number killed or wounded was believed to be 498. Honours awarded comprised one Victoria Cross, six Distinguished Conduct Medals, twenty-two Military Medals, one French *Croix de Guerre* and numerous Mentions in Despatches.

Proposals for honouring the fallen led to the establishment of a War Memorial Committee whose first meeting considered several forms of memorial. The suggestions included an extension to the infirmary, a new operating theatre, a small museum or a permanent roll of honour based on the town's coat of arms. All were declined as the committee considered they were not in a position to go into the permanency or form of the memorial. An agreement was finally made in 1924!

Far less lethargic were the Wigan Motor Volunteers, by late October they had made over thirty journeys and conveyed over 930 wounded during the year. They made ten journeys carrying about 150 men from the railway stations to the various Red Cross Hospitals. Entertainers from the Hippodrome were also taken to the hospitals where they provided free entertainment for the wounded. Despite petrol shortages,

American and British Red Cross women alongside one of the ambulance train carriages on exhibition in Wigan.

the squadron took the wounded on outings to Rivington, Parbold, Apply Bridge, Burscough and Southport etc.

The long haul evacuation of the wounded required the services of hospital ships and ambulance trains. The Lancashire and Yorkshire Railway Company was one of the first to produce an ambulance train to War Office specification and subsequent orders followed. Their latest ambulance train for use on the Continent was placed on view at the following stations: Wigan on 14 November, Southport on 15 November and Liverpool on 16 November. The train included 'all the latest devices for the expeditious and easy movement of wounded soldiers from the firing line'. The ten-coach train was open for inspection at the goods wharf of the Lancashire and Yorkshire station from 11 to 7pm. Admission tickets were 1s, and all monies collected financed comforts for British and American soldiers and sailors.

The railways were operating to full capacity but waterways were underused; the Leeds and Liverpool Canal Company had fifty canal boats lying idle and to ease rail congestion the company, in conjunction with the Army, trained military transport workers in boatmanship. As the 15th and 16th Prince of Wales's Volunteers (South Lancashire Regiment) battalions had men of low medical categories working in Mersey docks, presumably the boat crews were drawn from these battalions.

The trial involved a steam tug leaving the Liverpool wharf towing six barges laden with 250 tons of mixed cargo destined for Leeds. A unique feature of the half-mile long convoy was that the boats were worked by twenty men under a sergeant and an experienced captain – six having been appointed for this purpose. The steamer was fitted out as a floating billet and halted at night time, the first stop being Burscough, followed by a 13 November overnight at Wigan. They departed next morning with a puppy given as a mascot. The week-long induction course to Leeds involved negotiating 500 bridges and locks and the experiment was evidently successful for in April 1918 the South Lancashire Regiment raised the 17th (Transport Workers) Battalion which worked on canals linking the ports with industrial areas.

No less busy were the local allotment holders. Of these only forty-four responded to a Wigan Council food production survey indicating they had marginally eased the food crisis by producing 402cwt of potatoes, 416lbs of peas, 391lbs of beans, 2,530 turnips, 2,654 cabbage, 806 cauliflower, 653 beetroots, 1,728 celery and quantities of carrots, marrows, parsnips etc. Every ton of home produce was a ton less imported at the risk of life and limb to mercantile marine personnel.

Amongst those wounded in action was S. Howard, previously an overlooker at the mill of the Sandbrook Spinning Company, Orrell, he wrote to a friend:

'Just a few lines hoping this finds you quite well, as I am alright at present, only a little weak through loss of blood. I daresay you will be surprised to know I have landed in Blighty. You will see by the address I am at Brighton, which appears to be quite a nice place, but I have not been out the hospital yet. While I was at [censored] in France there was a fellow came down from the trenches almost dead through loss of blood. The doctor wanted a volunteer to give blood to him, so I volunteered to give him blood, and I had 1½ pints taken from my arm, and I now have four stitches in my arm, but I do not mind so long as I am on this side of the water.

I don't suppose it will be long before I shall be right again, but I am in no hurry, as I don't want France again if I can help it. We went over on 31 July, and it happened that me and the Lewis gun team were in the front line and in the German trenches first. It was 4am when we went over, and immediately we showed our head above the parapet there was a continuous stream of machine-gun bullets flying about. I saw scores of fellows put out, but what there was left of us went on, and reached the German snipers, and it happened we got round a bunch of them who had been and were knocking our fellows out. As soon as they saw they were cornered they surrendered. . . This happened at Ypres, which is the worst part of the whole line.'

Adverse weather had conspired against the British Third Ypres offensive which had failed to gain its key objectives, namely the liberation of the Belgian ports of Zeebrugge and Ostend and the capture of Roulers military railhead. Undeterred, the British launched the Battle of Cambrai, an ambitious scheme to pierce the Hindenburg Line strongpoints south-east of Arras, cross the St Quentin canal, seize the Cambrai railhead and capture Bourlon Ridge. The blows would fall on a 5-mile front and involve the first en masse deployment of 476 tanks.

The battle commenced on 20 November and the 'shock and awe' of tanks trundling over trenches stunned the Germans. But the success of the first few days waned as the British were unable to maintain momentum due to a shortage of infantry reserves, mechanical failure and the vulnerability of lumbering tanks to German short range artillery. A series of German counter-attacks typified the Teutonic ability to redress the balance and once again neither belligerent could produce the winning card; the fighting continued into December.

Our Russian ally had descended into civil war and anarchy; consequently on 16 December an armistice was signed on the Eastern Front, thus releasing German troops to prosecute the war on the Western Front. As victory hung in the balance, for the warring nations there was little goodwill and peace on earth as the fourth wartime Christmas approached.

The 66th (2nd East Lancashire) Territorial Division proceeded to France in late February.

CHAPTER 5

1918
The Final Blows

The New Year looked promising as expectations were high that the great untapped human reservoir of the keen but inexperienced American Expeditionary Force would restore numerical superiority before Germany could fully complete the transfer of troops from east to west. But, Germany was one step ahead, a wealth of preordained plans had been gathering dust in German headquarters for some time; one such plan, code named Operation Michael, was adapted for a spring offensive. In the meantime British strategy changed from offensive to defensive, confidently believing they could repulse any attempted German breakthrough. The distant Royal Navy blockade continued to exert an ever-tightening stranglehold on German imports, leading to civil unrest among the malnourished civilian population.

Although food shortages in Britain were less severe, week by week restrictions on the supply of food increased in severity. In Wigan and district, due to shortages, butter and margarine were restricted to ¼lb per person, bacon was becoming increasingly scarce and since the war began milk had doubled in price and the supply failed to meet demand. In mid-January the Wigan Food Control Committee requisitioned a supply of margarine imported from Holland to be divided amongst shops in the Market Place area. Large queues were reported due to 'certain unpatriotic and greedy families obtaining far more margarine than a few weeks ago, by sending more than one family member to queue, or by the same person going to many shops'. To alleviate the problem the food control committees in the Wigan area announced from 23 January supplies of margarine or butter would not be obtainable from any retailer in Wigan and district except on production of a sugar card for every member of the family or a soldier or sailor's leave pass.

Other uniformed men had been deliberating on enhancing the air raid precautions in the county of Lancashire Police Districts. In late January the public were advised that warning of the approach of hostile aircraft between thirty minutes before sunrise to thirty minutes after sunset were now in force. Sirens of various industrial and public establishments would give three blasts of fifteen seconds followed by one long blast of a minute; this would be repeated after a few minutes. The all clear would sound for one minute followed by a short blast.

Also amended was the successful rationing scheme now extended to a temporary scheme to abolish queues for butchers' meat, bacon or ham, and cheese. This affected more than a quarter of a million residents. On 18 February the food control committees of the borough of Wigan, the rural areas of Wigan, and the urban districts of Abram, Ashton-in-Makerfield, Aspull, Billinge, Hindley, Ince, Orrell, Standish and Up Holland brought the following restrictions into operation:

'No person is now permitted to sell or buy butchers' meat (which includes game, poultry, rabbits and sausages), bacon (or ham), and cheese, except on production of a ration card, and if supplies are available the weekly purchases of each person must not exceed 1s 6d worth of butchers' meat, three ounces of bacon or ham, and two ounces of cheese. A special card was issued to meet the requirements of caterers, institutions and manufacturers.'

This was a temporary measure pending a permanent rationing scheme. To alleviate the milk shortage, Wigan Corporation purchased a twenty-one cow dairy farm and extensive pasture land at Hoscar Moss, Lathom, near Ormskirk. The milk was despatched every morning from Hoscar Moss station to Wigan, a distance of about 7 miles. In late February the first consignment was distributed direct to the consumer at a reasonable price.

A parody on meat rationing.

The authorities were vigilant against any profiteering and to counter this 'on the ration' consumables had a set retail price. One such case involved Benedict Turner, wholesale butcher of Woodstock Street, who was summoned on 28 February at Wigan for thirty-six instances of contravening the Maximum Meat Price Order, 1917. Of these eighteen cases were for charging more than the scheduled price, another eighteen were fictitious wholesale entries in his book.

The defendant sold quantities of meat at 1s 1½d per pound when the maximum should have been 1s 5/8d per pound. The defence argued he had purchased cattle at enhanced prices, so that by supplying retail butchers he had lost in the transaction thus negating the shortage of meat and avoiding trouble. After lengthy consideration, the magistrate, in deference to the service of the defendant who was on the food committee, ordered the butcher to pay costs in the cases for exceeding maximum prices, plus a fine of £1 in each of the eighteen fictitious entries, amounting to £22 10s in all. Similar offences of food retailers profiteering (overcharging) or diluting milk were not uncommon.

A major loss to the community occurred when Mary, Lady Gerard unexpectedly died following a paralytic seizure. The late commandant of the Garswood Hall Military Hospital had recently been instrumental in the inauguration of a new district of the Red Cross Association for the Ashton-in-Makerfield district. The funeral took place on 23 February, and as the deceased had done so much to alleviate the suffering of servicemen, she received a military funeral with her coffin mounted on a gun carriage. A few weeks later, her daughter, who wished to maintain her mother's legacy, accepted the chairmanship of the Ashton Division of the BRCS. They had an ambulance donated and were financially maintained by Lancashire miners.

Early that morning Corporal Thomas Woodcock VC returned to Wigan.

'News had leaked out he was coming, and a great crowd of munition workers, cotton operatives and miners took time off and assembled on Wigan station platform. As the train steamed into the station loud cheers were raised, and an immediate rush along the carriages was made to find the gallant soldier. Great hurrahs heralded his detraining. . .'

The hero was met by the Mayor, Mayoress, Deputy Mayor, Town Clerk and council members on behalf of the fund which was being formed for Corporal Woodcock. The Mayor expressed the pride Wigan felt in having such a gallant soldier as a citizen, an afternoon civic reception followed.

On 2 March at the Pavilion, Wigan the Mayor presented Woodcock VC with an illuminated address and £150 in War Bonds. The hero, who was received with enthusiastic cheers, modestly disclaimed credit for having done anything that any other soldier would not have accomplished if put to the test.

Wigan munitionettes attend a Buy War Bonds meeting. (WA&LS).

Woodcock soon returned to front line duties where wily Lloyd George, with one eye on home front productivity and the other on servicemen casualties, had, for some time, been restricting the flow of men to France. During February British infantry divisions on the Western Front were reduced from a twelve-battalion basis to nine battalion strong units.

In fiscal terms, the daily cost of the war to Britain was £6,384,000 prompting King George to state:

'I am confident my people are willing to contribute, both now, and in the future, whatever money may be necessary to secure victory'.

The Chancellor of the Exchequer, Andrew Bonar Law, adopted a different tack:

'I should like those at the head of great financial institutions to convert to whatever extent they can Treasury Bills and take out War Bonds instead. The second thing I want the people of this country to do is save every penny they can of expenditure and lend their savings to the state.'

The country was asked to raise £100,000,000 in War Bonds and War Savings and every large town was set the task of providing funds for either a Dreadnought battleship (£2,500,000 each), a light cruiser (£400,000), a monitor (£250,000) a destroyer (£150,000), a submarine (£100,000) or an aeroplane (£2,500 each). The National War Savings effort known as Business Men's Week commenced 4 March. Wigan failed in the attempt to meet by the sales of War Bonds and certificates the hypothetical value of a monitor – basically a floating naval gun platform. The week began well with the Prudential Insurance Company investing £12,000 and overall the week's investments amounted to £133,000.

Also in early March the Home Secretary announced that 50,000 miners would be 'combed out', all exemption certificates issued on grounds of employment to persons in or about coalmines, who were on 22 November 1915 unmarried or widowed, were withdrawn without exemption. The men were to be chosen by age or ballot, a miner's leader claimed there was no undue rush to join the colours but felt the ballot was the means of a satisfactory solution.

Meanwhile General Ludendorff finalised plans for a major offensive between St Quentin on the Somme and the Arras sector, a battle front of almost 50 miles. The main blows would fall on the Anglo-French army boundary and inevitably create maximum confusion. After breaching the Allied line, German troops would then head north and sweep the under-strength British force into the sea. A decisive victory would have produced a similar result to the 1940 Fall of France. Douglas Haig reported sixty-four German divisions were amassed against twenty-nine British infantry divisions and three cavalry divisions, of which nineteen were in the line.

On 21 March the German spring offensive began, comprising four codenamed phases, the initial and most powerful being Operation Michael aimed at defeating the British on the Somme and compelling the French to seek an armistice. Operations Georgette, Gneisenau and Blücher-Yorck were designed to divert Allied forces from the Somme and reduce resistance. On the opening day of the offensive the Wigan raised 2/5 Manchester Battalion lost three-quarters of its strength and was later disbanded; the 5/Manchester were held in Divisional reserve. The static war suddenly became a war of mobility. Weakened Allied positions were over-run, the Fifth Army withdrew, in the process abandoning the Somme battlefields, but focusing their resources on the route to the Channel ports and the railhead at Amiens. Stiffening resistance and the rapid pace of the German advance prevented the replenishment of supplies and ammunition, the momentum of the advance was lost and the Allied crisis briefly abated.

The British had suffered 178,000 casualties, the French 92,000 but the Germans incurred 239,000 casualties, yet the fighting soon continued with renewed vigour in a desperate attempt to grasp the laurels of victory before significant American intervention.

The war claimed millions of lives including Margaret Roscoe (20), previously a healthy single woman and the daughter of Robert Roscoe, a collier of 85 Ladies Lane, Hindley. The Wigan Borough Coroner heard she had left home the previous July to work as a filler at a munitions factory, by September she was suffering from TNT poisoning and spent a fortnight in hospital until the 4 October Munitions Factory disaster (White Lund, Morecambe). Her nerves were shattered by the explosion and she returned jaundiced, almost black and complaining of feeling very poorly. For a fortnight she was attended by a doctor but her condition deteriorated, on 22 March she was admitted to the Infirmary and died on 1 April. A post mortem revealed a change in all her organs consistent with TNT poisoning, the cause of death being anaemia following on toxic jaundice due to TNT poisoning.

Other munition workers had less hazardous occupations including the employees at the Dorning Street clothing factory of Messrs Coop and Company. According to the *Wigan Examiner*, 'work tables were loaded with khaki uniforms and discharged soldiers clothing of all kinds, while huge piles reaching almost to the roof were ready for the nimble fingers of the girls at the machines.'

Others were involved in countless charitable associations, such as the Hindley Soldiers' and Sailors' Wives and Mothers Association whose latest fundraiser took place on 20 March. The women, assisted by the St John VAD 5091 Comforts Section, organised a concert where almost seventy children of the Argyle Street Independent Methodist School performed a cantata representing Britain and the Dominions. The concert proceeds were donated to the 700 bed military base hospital at Etaples which was raised through voluntary subscriptions of £75,000.

Coops' workers in Mesnes Park.

Hospitalisation through wounds is preferable to being killed in action, a fate that befell one of the town's most recognisable servicemen. On 3 April Mrs Woodcock of 2, Teck Street Wigan received a letter from Sergeant T. Murray advising that her husband had been killed in France. Accompanying the letter was a bloodstained photograph of Mrs Woodcock and their three young children.

Inside St Patrick's Church, Hardybutts, Wigan a brass plaque commemorates the fallen hero thus: 'In proud memory of Lance Corporal Thomas Woodcock Victoria Cross, Irish Guards. Born Wigan 1888. Killed in action Bullecourt, France 27 March 1918. *Quis Separabit.*'

On 27 June 2014 the *Manchester Evening News* reported Wigan had committed to honouring the town's four Victoria Cross recipients. Thomas Woodcock, John Grimshaw, William Keneally and Alfred Wilkinson from Leigh will each have a road named in their honour. The first road being Wilkinson Park Drive located on the site of Bickershaw Colliery where Wilkinson VC once worked. In 2015, the Ashton-in-Makerfield children's library was renamed in honour of Keneally VC.

Back in 1918, on 8 April the National Scheme for rationing meat came into force; this replaced the temporary Wigan scheme and covered all kinds of butchers' meat including pork, offal, suet, bacon, ham, sausages, poultry and game, (including birds of all kinds killed for food), hares, rabbits, venison, horseflesh and cooked, canned, preserved foods of all kinds. The food controller also prohibited the use of eggs for anything other than human consumption.

I CANNOT SEND YOU BANKNOTES,
I CANNOT SEND YOU GOLD,
BUT THIS SUGAR AND POTATO
ARE MORE THAN WEALTH UNTOLD.

A postcard lamenting the scarcity of potatoes and sugar.

Food rationing and air raids are now more associated with the Second World War but these experiences were endured by a previous generation. Airship *L61* crossed the coast at Withernsea, and at an altitude of 18,000ft crossed the Mersey at Malton. The first bomb damaged a sandstone milestone on the A57 Prescot to Warrington

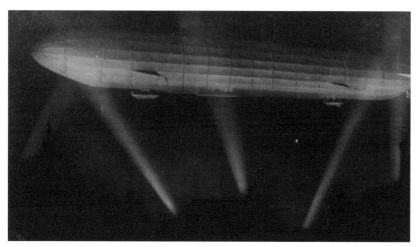

The low down thing that plays the low down game.

Road. A few minutes later at 11.20pm a second bomb exploded in a field at Abbots Hall Farm, Bold. The airship then headed in the general direction of Wigan.

Under wartime censorship the immediate newspaper reporting of the raid comprised – 'An air raid attended with the loss of five lives and considerable injury to various persons, as well as some damage to house property took place on Friday night in the north western district when one or more airships crossed from the eastern coast.'

Apart from a prompt coroner's inquest the publication of raid details were suppressed until after the Armistice when accounts appeared in the 20 December 1918 *Liverpool Daily Post* and the 1 April 1919 *Wigan Observer.* These primary sources give an insight into the terrifying minutes when Wigan unexpectedly experienced the wrath of Germany in what transpired to be the second Lancashire and the last effective airship raid.

At 10.40pm on 12 April, Wigan Police received news from private sources that one or more enemy aircraft were passing over North Yorkshire, but there was no mention of airships over Lancashire. In Wigan everything was as normal, the main thoroughfares were lit and the illumination of the Wigan Coal and Iron Company blast furnaces, in addition to several others, were visible from 20 miles. Police special constables were in the process of carrying out the routine precautions of warning householders to extinguish lights unaware a raider was in the immediate vicinity. Just before midnight the whirring drone of machinery was heard overhead when

'like a hawk from the darkness above the raider swooped down on the Wigan area and dropped about twenty-two bombs as it circled round. . . The explosion of the bombs, which fell with the most terrible consequences in the eastern portion of the district, could be heard for miles. Bombs fell in Wigan, Ince and in Aspull before the unmolested airship disappeared as mysteriously and as suddenly as it had come'.

Near the Ince boundary, a bomb demolished three houses and killed outright Samuel Tompkinson (49) and his wife Jane (58) of 37 Harper Street. They, along with the bedding and furniture, were blown some distance away into a deep hollow on some waste ground. A short distance away in Darlington Street East, a spent incendiary bomb lay on the footpath. Also in the Ince district, an unexploded bomb was said to have been seen on a railway cabin; a little further away a house in Preston Street was set on fire.

Two local hotels were considerably damaged, the former Von Blücher Hotel and the Birkett Bank Hotel. Rows of cottages in the vicinity of Scholfield Lane were peppered by shrapnel, while huge craters were made in the roadways. In several streets hardly a window was intact, Cecil Street for instance, having practically all the front bay windows wrecked and at Birkett Bank a gas lamp was thrown down and the escaping gas was blazing at the mains.

A collier named William Harris (29), of 181 Whelley was in the act of carrying his baby son to a place of safety when they were both killed on the staircase. A witness said he was in bed when he heard a loud explosion. He went outside and heard four explosions in quick succession. A bomb which exploded 50yds away blew him into the house. He heard someone down the street shouting for help, and saw that the back of a house had been blown out. He and another man climbed through a window and found Harris covered in blood (he was disembowelled) and he died forty-minutes later. The decapitated body of his four-month-old son Alfred was later found in the wreckage.

At 156 Platt Lane, Margaret Ashurst and her four-month-old son were asleep in bed when an explosion killed the mother. Her 12-year-

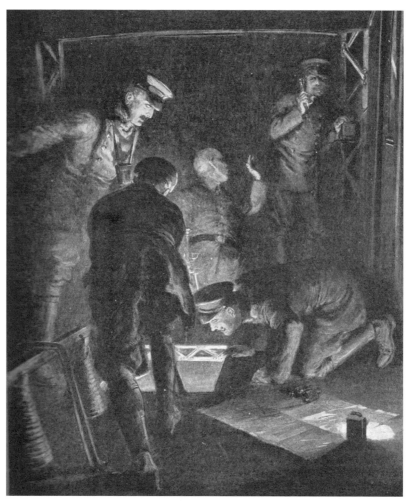

Germans dropping cone shaped bombs onto targets below.

old son later informed the coroner that when a neighbour called him and two siblings into a cellar his mother did not speak. Immediately there was another explosion which blew the windows and doors in. The neighbour stated that after the 'all clear' was given the mother was found with the lower part of her face blown away. The baby was in bed suffering from injuries to the head and bruises to the face. The bed adjoined a window overlooking the street, and the woman's head was towards the window.

In another house an unexploded bomb dropped on the empty bed of a miner working on the night shift, the householder attempted to

Children explore a Cecil Street bomb crater.

retain the bomb as a souvenir and his house gradually filled with curious neighbours. He had to be threatened with the penalties of the DORA before he parted with his dangerous souvenir.

The conduct of the inhabitants was admirable, there being no panic, though hundreds turned out, and made their way in darkness to the damaged areas. While the raid was in progress George Walker, the licensee of the Walmsley Arms Hotel, Lower Ince went to the local police station with an offer to help during the emergency. A mounted constable was preparing to go on duty and accidentally discharged his revolver; the bullet hit Walker in the abdomen and he died twenty minutes later.

The bombs killed five people outright, but in addition a man named Bolton was blinded by the explosion and Jane Winter of 6 Harper Street, Wigan died in the Wigan Union Workhouse on 19 April from pneumonia accelerated by shock owing to enemy aircraft. A coroner's jury returned a verdict of misadventure on all six persons who had met their deaths through bombs falling from an aircraft. The foreman added that the jury were of the opinion that someone was guilty of gross neglect in not giving warning of the approach of enemy aircraft. Another victim was Mrs Mary Cumberbirch (22) of 122 Schofield Lane, Wigan who was sitting at home when she was fatally injured about the head and shoulder and died in Wigan Infirmary on 21 April, nine days later.

The morning after the raid revealed a trail of devastation and the pitiful sight of survivors picking through the ruins of their homes or grieving their dead. An irate Wigan Council sent a letter to the Secretary of State complaining about the lack of a field marshal's warning and a lack of anti-aircraft defences. The badly shaken public confidence received a boost by the timely arrival of a morale raising iron mastodon.

The tank, Drake (137), commanded by Lieutenant A.E. Renwick MC, a veteran of the Battle of Cambrai, was one of the ironclads now used to promote War Bonds. On completion of its duties in Rochdale the tank arrived in Wigan on Sunday 14 April and gave a demonstration of its power and adaptability in climbing obstacles before taking up position at the corner of Woodstock Street and Market Street (by the old Market Hall). The next day Wigan launched their Tank Bank Week aimed at raising a highly optimistic £1,000,000 in War Bonds equivalent to £4 per head of the local population.

The business bank tank.

The Mayor of Wigan officially opened the tank bank and invested for the corporation an initial £30,000. As an additional incentive to patriotism a prize of a 15s 6d War Savings Certificate was given for every investment in gold of £20 or over, this led to £900 in gold passing through the bank in one day. The Pemberton Miners' Association invested £4,000, the Prudential Assurance Company £10,000 and the Pearl Assurance Company also £10,000, while other businesses, local miners' trade unions, cotton operatives and all other workers invested all their available funds. Mr Harry Twist, miners' agent, who was the first Labour MP returned for Wigan, conducted a tour of the mines to address the men as they left the pits at 'black face' meetings and a total of £29,468 was raised from Wigan school pupils. The Tank Bank week accrued Post Office investments of £581,940; this was considered a satisfactory response, Drake then departed for St Helens.

Workplaces were now routinely checked for men carrying out work that could be done by women. The quest for men expanded its parameters in April when the Military Service Act extended compulsory military service to 51-year-olds. And in May, regardless of their occupation, any men born in 1898-99 were called up. The military dispensation for male war production workers was reviewed and by mid-1918 yielded a further 100,000 conscripts.

There was a shortage of potatoes due to three-quarters of the crop going to the military. To alleviate the shortage Wigan Corporation purchased two tons of scarce seed potatoes which were sold to allotment holders from a temporary shop in Tower Buildings and a quantity were planted in parks.

On 6 May Wigan Corporation decided to establish and maintain an experimental municipal kitchen in the borough in keeping with National Food Kitchens and the coal controller's insistence on fuel economy. The non-profit-making kitchens provided inexpensive meals. The customers generally provided their own crockery and took the food home. Typically a family of two adults and two children could buy a meal of potatoes and gravy for 6d, but if the adults required meat, the price rose to 9d. The scheme also reduced individual demand for rationed products.

But the overriding shortage continued to be soldiers, Sir Auckland Geddes, director of National Service circulated a letter to local authorities increasing pressure on military tribunals to produce more recruits:

A romantic postcard complete with mistletoe posted by a husband on active service on 27 May 1918 to his wife, Mrs S. Atherton, 27 William Street, Lower Ince.

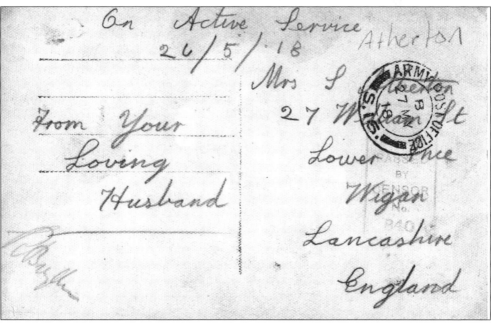

'At the present critical stage of the war even greater efforts and sacrifices than those already made are necessary on the part of all classes of the community. The demand for men in the higher medical grades or categories is insistent, and must be met at once if the national forces are to be maintained in adequate strength. No fit man of fighting age should now receive exemption on occupation grounds unless he is engaged on work directly important to the prosecution of the war. There is a general paramount necessity that an increased flow of fit men should be obtained without delay to furnish His Majesty's Forces the support which is essential'.

However, Albert Ward who lived at 15 Shelton Street, Bryn thought differently. He was well known as a Sunday evening political speaker on Wigan Market Square. On 7 July his audience heard 'our lads are being slaughtered for the French', and also 'why are our lads being slaughtered for the French capitalists'. He was accused of contravening DORA Regulations by making statements by word of mouth to prejudice His Majesty's relations with foreign powers. He was also accused of making statements to prejudice the training, discipline or administration of His Majesty's Forces. The local authorities sought

The band of the Ashton-in-Makerfield Convalescent Hospital.

permission from the military authorities to proceed with the case, but for inexplicable reasons the necessary permission was extensively delayed.

Meanwhile on the Western Front in a series of bitterly contested engagements the Allies reversed German fortunes. On 15 July, near Reims, Ludendorff launched his final great offensive but made little progress. Three days later, a Franco-American counter-attack supported by masses of light tanks drove back the Germans. Depleted of reserves and weakened by 50,000 casualties, on 20 July Ludendorff abandoned his Flanders offensive and went on the defensive.

Over one and a quarter million American Expeditionary Force men were now in France and, although inexperienced, their presence had a demoralising effect on German forces' morale. Allied counter-attacks were many, but the most significant of the final blows occurred near Amiens on 8 August. The surprise Anglo-French attack broke against a demoralised enemy increasingly fighting without conviction. General Ludendorff later described 8 August as 'the black day of the German Army in the history of the war… it put the decline of our fighting power beyond all doubt'.

The Allied advance to victory had begun which may have given some consolation to Wigan folk as hundreds queued on Saturday afternoons for ½oz of tobacco. Germany occupied large sectors of French industrial areas including coalfields. In an age when 'coal was king' Britain exported her own precious coal for use in French industry and warships. The combing out of miners and high demand for coal created a domestic coal shortage. Billposter boards throughout Wigan and district notified customers of the necessity to return their coal rationing forms to their preferred coal merchant before coal rationing became effective on 21 September. New ration books were scheduled for release in the middle of October.

Later that month, Albert Ward appeared in court charged with five offences committed on 7 July, and 15 and 22 September when he made false statements in speeches delivered at the Market Square. The defendant addressed the court for ninety-minutes when he admitted some of the remarks but asserted his right to free speech. His line of defence perturbed the court their verdict was postponed for ten days, then another week. After much angst over the issue of freedom of speech, Ward was sentenced to six months imprisonment and a £100 fine plus court costs; free speech had become another war casualty.

Meanwhile, in Europe the German tide began to ebb and gradually withdrew in the direction of the Fatherland. Ludendorff admitted the war could not be won, but wished to maintain a strong military position to negotiate favourable terms in the inevitable peace treaty, ideally retaining possession of Belgium and Luxemburg. Austria promised to send reinforcements to France, but a few weeks later attempted to broker a peace deal with the United States; it was declined. On 27 September Bulgaria also sought an armistice, followed by the abdication of their monarch, and in the same month the Turkish army in Palestine was defeated.

At home victory appeared as distant as ever. Due to rationing many Wigan consumers found they had exceeded their allowance of gas and from 22 October new ration books were exchanged for existing ones. Despite rationing, the Sailors' and Soldiers' Rest Rooms managed to serve 5,500 visitors a week with cost price food. No charge was made for use of the billiard table, cleaning clothes or care of kits and valuables, and many of the 170 voluntary staff were qualified Red Cross workers, who could if necessary dress and attend the wounded. On 8 November this war charity launched a week-long series of collections at colleries, mills, factories and churches, meanwhile world events neared conclusion.

Faced with the collapse of the alliance between the Central Powers, Germany became increasingly isolated prompting Ludendorff to demand an armistice, to which the Kaiser agreed. On 5 November the Admiralty announced they had successfully defeated the submarines and maintained a huge convoy system. Of the 85,772 merchant ships convoyed only 433 were lost. Germany's key allies Turkey and Austria-Hungary signed armistices on 30 November and 3 November respectively. Her own peace negotiations stalled over President Wilson's insistence on the abdication of Kaiser Wilhelm II.

Exasperated by the Kaiser's reluctance, the German Chancellor forced the Kaiser's hand by announcing his abdication on 9 November (he officially abdicated on 28 November). Two days later Germany signed an armistice signifying a ceasefire with effect from the eleventh hour of the eleventh day of November.

When the news reached Wigan an official communication was forwarded immediately to the Mayor who was employed at Pemberton

Flag bedecked buildings in Wallgate.

Colliery. The glad tidings spread like wildfire and the townspeople, moved by patriotic fervour, left homes, shops or mills and surged to the centre of town to vent their jubilation that the struggle of the Allies had been carried to a triumphant conclusion. Flags, chiefly Union Jacks, were thrust through the uppermost widows of central buildings and as the crowds increased flags of all sizes and patriotic ribbons appeared by the hundred. The national flag flew from the tower of the Parish Church shortly followed by outbursts of the peals of victory from the bells as if in competition with the mill buzzers and sirens spreading the good tidings. The street crowds were soon reinforced by the thousands of women engaged in the various mills and munition works. At midday the tramcar employees returned their cars to the depot and took the remainder of the day as a holiday. At 2pm the Mayor, Alderman Cheetham, councillors and other dignitaries assembled at the Borough Court where a large crowd had gathered outside. Speaking from the main entrance steps his worship informed the public there would a procession to the Market Square.

From the Market Hall steps the Mayor said he was pleased to inform the people that he had received an official telegram notifying that the Armistice had been signed at 5am that morning. After various speeches the mayoral party proceeded to the Parish Church where a thanksgiving service was held. Throughout the afternoon and evening scenes of jubilation, there were no incidents of horseplay or rowdiness instead a sense of disbelief and gratitude to the gallant men who had delivered the great victory prevailed.

Warfare on the Western Front had ceased but elsewhere the war continued. A military machine and supporting infrastructure assembled in excess of four years would take time to dismantle before life returned to normal and families and communities recovered from apocalyptic warfare. Men optimistically posted as missing were presumed dead, but with no identified remains families usually waited in vain for glad tidings concerning their loved one. The military began to demobilise, priority being given to miners and other occupations so desperately needed at home. This caused great resentment to men who had signed up for a period designated 'duration of war only' and for most it would be early spring before they returned home. The wounded still needed tending, there would be no remarkable peacetime recovery, and indeed legions would die for decades from Great War injuries.

Past battle honours are traditionally displayed on regimental colours, the colours of the 5/Manchester were presented to the battalion in July 1909, by King Edward VII at Worsley and since the outbreak of the Great War had been deposited in the Parish Church. On 16 December 1918, the colours were handed to a specially appointed escort party, to be transferred to the battalion headquarters 'somewhere in France'. The Rector, Canon Matthew, handed the colours to the Mayor who presented them to Lieutenant Rotteneau and Second Lieutenant Wright. This was followed by a state procession and public function, when references were made to the gallant deeds and unflinching bravery for which so many gallant Wigan lads had sacrificed their lives.

The town's financial contribution was acknowledged when the Wigan War Savings Committee received a letter on 25 March 1919 from the National War Savings Committee advising that the Army Council had placed at their disposal a large number of tanks for presentation to towns with a population exceeding 10,000 whose record

A forlorn collection of flags and standards inside the parish church. The regimental colours of the 5/Manchester, too fragile to touch, are on the extreme left.

in financing the war reached a level of patriotic achievement as entitled them to enjoy this distinction. Wigan was thus offered a tank, which would not only permanently commemorate the notable achievement of its citizens in financing the war, but also bear lasting testimony to the important part played by the Wigan War Savings Committee in this

COPYRIGHT E.L.P.C?   ONE OF OUR TANKS   PASSED BY CENSOR

A First World War tank

country's war effort. It was not possible to give a date of the tank's arrival; the offer, deemed of the highest civic importance, was gratefully accepted by the civic authorities.

Councillors were still in disagreement over the most appropriate form of war memorial, a stop gap measure being a temporary war shrine in the form of a cross erected on a hill in Mesnes Park and unveiled in July 1919, by the Mayor, John Cheetham JP.

At the next council meeting the Mayor and peers were read a letter from the War Office Trophies Committee dated 19 August offering Wigan a damaged German machine-gun together with mountings and ammunition belt – the offer was declined by councillors. A letter from Lieutenant Colonel W.J. Woodcock 16/Lancashire Fusiliers was also read aloud advising that he was allocating some German field guns captured by his battalion and offered two to Wigan which the committee gladly accepted.

At the next council meeting the rejected machine gun was on display in the committee room. An indignant Town Clerk informed

councillors he had forwarded a letter to the War Trophies Committee '. . .that this town was worthy of some better consideration in way of war trophies than the one that had been sent, and impressing on them the importance of giving special consideration to this large community'.

The two German howitzers were placed in Mesnes Park on 21 November 1919 and on 20 January they were joined by the promised tank whose engine was offered to the Wigan and District Mining and Technical College for purpose of exhibition and tuition. The offer was declined. Shortly after the tank's arrival, railings were erected around it to protect it from the attentions of children who found it an excellent plaything.

But, it was not only weaponry that was surplus to requirement – Billinge Auxiliary Military Hospital had treated 5,000 patients, the last of whom were discharged on 29 May 1919.

Following the closure of the Woodlands Hospital Group a hospital flag accompanied with a modest brass plaque was presented to the care of Wigan Parish Church. Another flag with a grander commemorative plaque was also ceremoniously presented to St Wilfred's Church, Standish.

Also in 1919, the Wigan Infirmary Extension Fund received over

1919	WIGAN & DISTRICT DIVISION OF THE BRITISH RED CROSS SOCIETY, PER HAROLD SUMNER O.B.E.	1862:3:4 & WARD EQUIPMENT
1920	MR & MRS JAMES BROWN.	1000
	COMMITTEE OF CARSWOOD HALL AUXILIARY HOSPITAL, PER LADY GERARD.	276:17:0
1920	MEMBERS OF BRYN BRANCH LANCASHIRE COUNTY WAR COMFORTS' ASSOCIATION	100:12:6

The infirmary extension fund donations and legacies were recorded for posterity on marble plaques and are still displayed within the hospital.

£1,862 plus ward equipment from the Wigan and District Division of the BRCS following the closure of the War Service Division.

The following year the fund received over £276 from the Committee of Garswood Hall Auxiliary Hospital and just over £100 from the members of the Bryn Branch of the Lancashire County War Comforts Association.

Disagreement continued over whether the war memorial should be an extension to the infirmary or a proposed art museum and whether the cost should be funded by ratepayers. At a public meeting held on 9 February 1922 a fresh committee relaunched the project and again the discussion centred on the precise form of memorial. The Mayor reminded the gathering that on being elected he had promised to raise a fund for a permanent memorial which would provide a focus for future Armistice days in the town. And, to gain public support and be representative of Wigan, it should not be funded out of the rates but by public subscription. In November the committee announced the preferred site for the memorial was at the entrance to the parish churchyard, and in what appears a compromise, a sum of £15,000 should be raised towards a war cross, with the balance going to a new operating theatre at Wigan Infirmary. The scheme required the partial demolition of the Dog and Partridge Hotel but this was opposed by the owners. The problem was resolved in February 1925 when the Diocese of Liverpool granted land in the churchyard.

Wigan Parish Church.

The memorial was designed by Sir Giles Gilbert Scott RA, the architect of Liverpool Cathedral, and cost £4,400 (excluding the council financed groundwork) the money being raised by public subscription. The memorial, designed on the lines of the old Eleanor Crosses, stands in the shadow of Wigan Parish Church in a portion of All Saints' Gardens. During the foundation excavations it was found necessary to disturb the long buried dead, their remains were re-interred at the four corners of the 22ft octagonal base. The 44ft high cross is surmounted with decorative carved leaf pinnacles with eight angels bearing wreaths symbolic of victory. The whole memorial is fashioned

The town War Memorial.

from Clipsham Stone, with the exception of the forty name panels which were originally of Hopton Wood marble, later replaced due to erosion.

On Saturday, 17 October 1925 at 3.30pm the memorial was unveiled by General the Honourable Sir Herbert Alexander Lawrence KCB and the dedication was by the Lord Bishop of Liverpool (The Right Reverend A.A. David DD). The Earl of Crawford, who was unable to attend the ceremony, sent a letter in which he paid high tribute to the endurance and heroism of the men during the war. Wreaths of remembrance were laid at the base by the Mayor of Wigan (Mr T. Holland), General Lawrence, Sir H.C. Darlington (who was Brigadier-General at Gallipoli), the officer commanding 5/Manchester, the two orphans of Woodcock VC and others. The poignant ceremony commemorated over 1,800 Wigan men who died in what was perceived then as the war to end all wars – but the names of subsequent generations would follow.

There was a postscript to the once much coveted tank, for in 1935, when German militarism was again raising concerns, the *Wigan Observer* reported:

> The tank, grim relic of the last war, which has been on exhibition in Mesnes Park since January 1920, along with the two field guns which have for years dominated the main entrance to the park from the pavilion terrace, have been sold for scrap to Mr J. Calderbank, metal broker of Woodhouse Lane, Wigan. The guns were removed by means of a crane and motor lorry on Thursday [27th June] and the tank is at present in process of being cut up by oxy-acetylene blow torch to facilitate removal.'

The tank and guns were considered 'unsightly objects in the park and served no useful or ornamental purpose'. The Markets and Parks committee received War Office permission to dispose of them on the proviso the scrap value of £40 was donated to charity. Presumably this was the town's final charitable donation relating to the Great War.

Selected Bibliography and Further Reading

Ancient and Loyal. Some *Wigan Review* extracts reprinted by Heyes and Company Ltd 1930.
County Borough of Wigan. Minutes of Council and Committees 1914 to 1919.
Mesnes Conservation Area Appraisal, The (2006).

Newspapers and Periodicals

Dundee Courier
Liverpool Daily Post
Liverpool Echo
Manchester Courier and Lancashire General Advertiser
Manchester Evening News
Wigan Observer and District Advertiser
Wigan Examiner
Yorkshire Evening Post

By the same author:

Wirral in the Great War
Liverpool in the Great War

Index